Crossing the River

Johnie N. Mozingo

© 2018

Preface

As a child and young woman, I became
fascinated with the numerous stories I heard about one
of my great grandmothers. I became convinced that
this remarkable woman deserved to be remembered in
some way other than a name on obscure census records
and a stone in a rarely visited family cemetery.
Eventually, I decided that if I didn't tell her story, it
likely would never be told.

Fortunately, when I first became interested in
this project, there were still living resources who have
long since departed this earth. My father (Teddie in the
book) spent the first fourteen years of his life in close
association with this special lady and was a source of
much valuable information long before I had any idea I
would write this book. An older cousin, the youngster
Helen in the book, was another wonderful resource.
Finally, there was a surprising amount of information
to be gleaned from wills, census records, slave
schedules, cemetery stones, and even old letters.

The names of most of the people in this book are
the actual names of long dead relatives. Unfortunately,

most of the slaves mentioned in the book had to be given fictitious names because only the gender and age of slaves were recorded on slave schedules. Only the names of the slaves George and Dick were passed down in family stories, but others such as "Lucy" were very real individuals even though their names are not known. In sum, this novel combines a little imagination and a lot of family history to tell what I believe to be a compelling story.

I would like to thank my dear friend Dr. Sally Blowers who graciously gave of her time to proof read the manuscript and provide suggestions. Maybe this book will be as rarely viewed as those obscure census records and the stone in a lonely cemetery, but it is my attempt to pay homage to a remarkable and courageous woman whose ancestry I am proud to claim.

Johnie N. Mozingo

Chapter 1

Lives Interrupted

August 1832

The anguished sobbing sounds coming from the parlor assaulted Mary's ears as she sat on the steps of the porch. At age eight, she didn't fully comprehend the finality of her mother's death but wished more than anything for her father's sobbing to stop. In the parlor lay the body of Mary's mother in a pine coffin set atop sawhorses draped with black cloth. A few neighbors and family members were trying without any success to console the grieving man who sat with arms clasped about himself as he swayed back and forth in the same chair he'd been in most of the night.

In the front yard, wagons and buggies stood at the ready for the five mile trip to the cemetery. Horses switched their tails at the annoyance of flies in the August sun. As Mary sat watching the horses, she covered her ears with her hands in an attempt to shut out the sounds of her father's pain. Her grandmother

Jane came and sat beside her on the steps. In silence, the old woman slipped an arm around Mary's shoulder. In spite of the August heat, Mary felt comforted by the gesture. After several moments, Mary felt her grandmother's arm slip away and heard her say, "Mary, it's almost time to leave for the cemetery. Put on this bonnet to shield you from the sun. The trunk containing your and Eliza's clothes is in the wagon that your Uncle Milton will be driving. You can ride with me in the buggy to the cemetery to keep your clothes fresh. Afterward you can ride your own pony that your daddy is sending with you to your Uncle Samuel's house. If you get tired, you can ride in the wagon."

Until two days prior, Mary had known nothing of the harsh realities that life sometimes offers. She was sheltered by two loving parents and an older sister she loved. Her mother took care of the house and the garden while her father handled things at his store in the little community of Graham's Chapel. Mary and eleven year old Eliza had chores to do and were expected to practice their needlework skills and participate in school lessons provided by their mother.

Their mother, originally from Baltimore, wanted her daughters to learn to be proper ladies.

On that fateful day two days prior, Mary's mother had complained of a headache and told Mary and her sister that she was going to lie down. Mary remembered those last words well. "My head is really hurting, and I'm going to lie down for a few minutes. If I should drop off to sleep, wake me at eleven. I'll need to fix some lunch for us."

Promptly at eleven, Mary went to wake her mother. "Mama, it's time to wake up." Mary waited for a response. Her mother lay on her side, arms cupped protectively around her eight-month pregnant belly. Mary spoke again and lightly shook her mother's upper arm.

Mary ran for Eliza. "There's something wrong with Mama. She won't wake up."

After Eliza also tried unsuccessfully to awaken their mother, she instructed Mary to go for their father. Mary dashed out the front door, slamming the screen as she went. Her feet sped across the yard as fast as she could run to the store. Paying no heed to the customer at the counter, Mary, now in tears, began to scream. "Daddy, Daddy, there's something wrong with Mama. She won't wake up."

Mary watched as her father's long legs took him quickly across the yard to the house. The customer, a neighbor Mary knew well, followed with Mary.

When Mary got to the bedroom, her daddy was already there, seated on the side of the bed, cradling his wife's head and loudly pleading "No! No! No!" Despite the anguished cries, the reality was clear. No pleading and no amount of tears would change anything. Death had called without warning to the Graham household.

Both Mary and Eliza stood in stunned silence. The neighbor was the first to speak. "William, I'm going to fetch my wife and some of the other neighbors. While I'm gone, you be deciding who you want notified."

Mary was the first to throw her arms around her father. Eliza followed. William Graham hugged his two little daughters back, and the three remained in a tight clutch until the neighbor returned, followed almost immediately by his wife, a bustling take-charge kind of woman who shooed the girls out of the room while announcing that a second lady who lived nearby was on her way. As the girls left the room, Mary heard the neighbor man ask again about who should be notified as he took Mary's father by the elbow and led him out. "I know your wife's family isn't from around here. Please try to pull yourself together, and tell me who needs to be notified."

Not knowing what else to do, Mary stood nearby as decisions were made about who should be notified of her mother's death. "My wife's parents in Sevier County should be notified as well as her brothers living in Grainger County. Someone will need to start for Grainger County right away to have daylight for the entire trip there. My own father will also need to be notified promptly because a grave will need to be dug in the family cemetery just down the road in Oak Grove."

The neighbor man led Mary's father out to the porch just as the second neighbor lady arrived. Having been sent out of the room once, Mary didn't try to re-enter, but through the partially open door she could hear the two women discussing what to put on the body. She heard one mention that a particular dress was pretty but would never button up the front because of the swollen belly. The take-charge lady said, "No problem! We'll just split the dress up the back." She stepped out of the bedroom then, and seeing Mary nearby, instructed her to find a pair of scissors.

After Mary provided the scissors, she went looking for Eliza who seemed to have disappeared. She found her sister sitting forlornly in the kitchen. Looking up, Eliza said "Mama's dead, Mary."

"I know, Eliza; I know." Then Mary sat down in numb silence with her sister.

Soon another neighbor lady arrived, bearing food, probably food she had prepared for her own family's noon meal. She portioned food out on two plates for the girls and set the plates before them. "Eat now. You've got to stay strong, and be a help to your daddy." Then the lady prepared a third plate and went to find William Graham.

After the girls had finished the meal, picking at the food more than actually eating it, they were invited by the take-charge lady to come see their mother. The body was now laid out neatly on the bed, dressed in the blue silk dress Mary had always liked on her mother. Mary thought her mother looked like she was sleeping and bent over to plant a soft kiss on the cheek. She touched her mother's hand and was shocked at how cold it felt.

Eliza, more aware of adult manners, thanked the ladies for their efforts and for making her mother look so peaceful and beautiful. She took Mary's small hand and whispered "Let's go find Daddy."

When the girls found their father, he was seated in a chair on the porch, the uneaten plate of food on the floor beside him, serving only to attract several flies. The neighbor man was still there but appeared to be getting ready to leave. Mary heard the man tell her father that riders had been found and would soon stop by for directions to the relatives' homes. He also said he would find another neighbor to help him carry the coffin from the store to the house. Mary saw tears well in her father's eyes then. Her mother would be buried in a coffin built by William himself. When he wasn't waiting on customers in the store, he often constructed coffins as a service for the community and for extra profit for the store.

As the day wore on, Mary and Eliza filled the hours with their usual chores. They washed the dishes from the noon meal, fed the chickens, swept the house and front porch, carried scraps from breakfast and lunch to the two pigs they were raising, and collected the eggs. Neighbors were in and out during the middle part of the day but then seemed to mostly disappear until near suppertime.

When Mary went to the front porch to sweep, she noticed that her father was no longer seated there. He wasn't in the house either, so Mary thought he must have gone back to the store. In a short while, her father returned with the neighbor man, the two of them bearing the coffin in which Mary's mother would be buried. William had gone to the store to select the coffin himself from several he had on hand.

When Mary saw the coffin again, it was on sawhorses in the parlor with her mother's body inside. Her father had returned to the chair on the porch, staring blankly out toward the store and the road.

About 5:00 p.m., Eliza suggested to Mary that the two of them should try to prepare something for supper. As they discussed what they might be able to prepare, two neighbor ladies showed up with food for the evening meal. One of the women nagged William until he finally joined Mary and Eliza at the table, but he mostly sat silently staring at the food or occasionally moving it around the plate with his fork. After a few minutes, he said, "Please excuse me, girls," and went back to the chair on the porch.

When the girls finished eating, they collected scraps for the hogs, washed the dishes, and carried the dishes back to neighbors who had brought the food. Afterward, they asked their father if there was anything they could do for him.

"No, I'm fine," replied William.

Hearing their father's negative response and with no chores remaining for the day, Eliza suggested to Mary that they get ready for bed. "What's going to happen tomorrow?" queried Mary.

"I don't know, Mary. I guess Grandma Jane will come sometime, and some of our uncles will come.

Neighbors will be in and out, like today. I heard one of the women say that ordinarily Mama would be buried tomorrow, but that she guessed that would be delayed for a day to give time for the kin to get here. Don't worry about it for now. We'll find out soon enough. Just get ready for bed."

The following day evolved much as Eliza had predicted. The girls prepared breakfast for themselves and their father, although once again he ate very little and said almost nothing during the meal. After the meal, he announced he was going to the store.

"Why, Daddy?" asked Eliza.

"Folks might need something," was his only reply. He looked to Mary like someone sleepwalking.

With Eliza giving directions, the two girls set about doing their morning chores, which consumed most of the morning. At one point, Mary asked Eliza if they should try to prepare a noon meal.

"We probably don't need to. I think some of the neighbors will bring food again. If they haven't brought anything by noon, we can think about something then. There's plenty in the garden and some cornbread left from last night."

Food did arrive as Eliza had predicted, and in mid-afternoon, their Grandmother Jane Shields came, accompanied by two of her neighbors. Grandpa James hadn't been up to the trip. After greeting the girls and giving them warm hugs, Grandma Jane asked where their father was. Her response to their answer was swift.

"At the store! Why's he at the store? Doesn't he know you two motherless children need some attention from him?" Without further comment, she announced, "I'm going to the store. I need to talk to your father."

Grandma Jane was gone for a long time, leaving Mary and Eliza to decide on their own what they should be doing. They decided to first check the garden for vegetables to pick, and when that was done, they checked the hens' nests for eggs.

Toward suppertime, two of the uncles, Uncle Samuel and Uncle Milton arrived, greeted the girls, and went to the store in search of their mother and brother-in-law. By the time all came back from the store, neighbors had again brought food, and two ladies brought flowers for the parlor. Several neighbors came to express sympathy and view the body. Mary overheard snatches of conversation about when they would leave for the cemetery the following morning and something about "avoiding heat of the day" and "travel time to Grainger County."

As one after another neighbor either expressed sympathy and left or took a seat in the parlor for the wake, William Graham's two-day composure came to an end. He sat down in a chair and began to sob.

Grandma Jane led the girls off to their room and began to explain what would happen the following day. "You'll need to be up early, washed and dressed by 7:30 or 8:00 a.m. at the latest. Neighbor ladies are bringing breakfast, and we're leaving at 9:00 a.m. for the cemetery. What the two of you haven't been told, and your father appears to be in no shape to tell you himself, is that you're going home with your Uncle Samuel. There's no way you two little girls can be expected to take care of the house and basically raise yourselves while your daddy is at the store all the time."

Eliza queried, "Will we be coming back here after Mama is buried?"

"No, you won't be coming back here afterwards. You'll be five miles on your journey to your Uncle Samuel's place, an all day trip. So we need to pack your clothes tonight except for what you'll sleep in and what you'll wear tomorrow. Now come give me a hug. I'm sad too. It's my precious daughter we're putting in the ground tomorrow."

Mary saw the tears on her grandmother's face and felt hot tears overflowing her own eyes. She hugged her grandmother for a long time before she started to gather clothes for packing.

When the packing was complete, Mary asked if there was room in the trunk for her favorite doll.

"Absolutely," replied her grandmother. "Your dolly might get very lonely if you leave her here."

Turning to Eliza, Grandma Jane asked if she had a doll or special toy she wanted to add to the trunk. "Even if you don't play with the doll anymore, you might want to take her along as a remembrance of home."

Mary was so tired after the long, busy day that she laid awake only a few minutes before she fell asleep wondering what the following day would bring.

Chapter 2

A New Life Begins

As Mary rode in the buggy with her grandmother, she wondered if her daddy had finally stopped sobbing. He was in a different buggy, driven by the same neighbor who had been so helpful on the day Mary's mother died. If he was still sobbing, at least Mary couldn't hear him now.

"Grandma, do you think my daddy is going to be all right? I've never once seen him cry before."

"Yes, I think your daddy will be all right. He's just a sensitive, caring man, and he loved your mother very much. It's good he's expressing his grief. Some men are afraid to do that. I think it was his sensitive and caring nature that made your mother want to marry him in the first place."

Mary thought for several seconds about her grandmother's words before asking another question. "So, with Eliza and me going to live at Uncle Samuel's place, who is going to cook and take care of the house for Daddy?"

"I don't know for sure, Mary, but your daddy is a resourceful man. He may pay a neighbor to clean the house and fix meals. I don't know. I do know that you don't need to be worrying your pretty little head about all that."

Mary rode in silence for several minutes before raising yet another question. "Do you think I'll like it at Uncle Samuel's place?"

"Yes, I think you'll like it at your Uncle Samuel's place. He's one of my children, too, you know. He's seven years younger than your mother, but they were always close. With eleven children in the house, the older ones always had to help with the younger ones, and your mother was just the right age to chase after Samuel when he was little and trying to get into everything. When he was older and had school lessons, your mother helped him with those. When he chose to study to be a doctor, your mother was so proud. He was educated in Baltimore before we moved south. You'll like your Aunt Eliza, too, and if you like to play with little children, there'll be plenty of that also. They have a three year old boy, John Howard, and a little girl, Mary Jane who is just a year old."

"That's going to be confusing to have an aunt with the same name as my sister and a baby with the same first name as mine."

"Don't worry about that. You'll figure out what to call everyone. Your aunt will, of course, always be 'Aunt Eliza,' and I think they always call the baby by her middle name."

Mary's chatter continued. "Mama was going to have a baby, you know."

"Yes, I know, and I know both your parents were excited about that. I think your daddy was hoping for a son this time, but he would have loved the baby, regardless, just like he loves you."

"Will Daddy come visit us at Uncle Samuel's? Can we visit him?"

"Mary, you are full of questions this morning, but I guess that's understandable…I wouldn't count on coming home to visit anytime soon if I were you; it's just too long a trip. I'm sure your daddy will come see you when he can. Maybe he can hire somebody to mind the store for him sometime. Also, I'm sure he'll write you letters."

"I'll like that, but it won't be like getting to see him all the time."

"That's true, Mary, but at least you still have a daddy. My father-in-law, , William Shields, arrived in this country as a nine year old orphan. His mother had died in Ireland, and both his father and brother died on the ship in route here. All alone in the new world, he had no choice but to become an indentured servant until he reached adulthood."

"What does that mean?"

"That means he had to work for someone for just a roof over his head and food to eat. He had a good mind though and applied himself well. As an adult, he became quite prosperous and provided well for his eleven children."

"Are we almost to the cemetery, Grandma?"

"I'm not sure, Mary; I'm not familiar with this road."

Mary was silent for a while, listening to the clip-clop of the horse's hooves as they struck the ground. In the distance, she could hear some angry crows arguing about something.

Suddenly, the little procession came to a halt. Soon, the neighbor man who had driven the buggy for Mary's father, approached their buggy. "The cemetery is up on the hill yonder, near that grove of trees." He pointed. "The hill is pretty steep. It wouldn't be safe to try to drive the buggy up there. Do you think you'll be able to walk up there, Ma'am?"

"I'll be fine, young man. If you'll just assist me down, I can walk up the hill with no problem."

As Mary and her grandmother walked up the hill, they were joined by Eliza. Several people were already gathered at the top of the hill near the clearly visible coffin sitting on the ground beside an open grave. The girls and their grandmother were the last to join the little group. Their grandfather Graham smiled and nodded at them as they arrived, and immediately the minister began the service.

Mary didn't comprehend everything the preacher said, but she heard him mention the date of her mother's birth in 1795 and her death on August 23, 1832. He extoled her many virtues, read some verses from the Bible, and then said something about her having "crossed the river." Those words immediately grabbed Mary's attention. She thought about her mother's story about a little boy who had drowned in the river and her warning to Mary and Eliza about staying away from the river near their home. This idea of her mother crossing a river worried Mary. As she focused on those thoughts, she realized that the preacher had just said "amen" and several men were lowering the coffin with ropes into the open grave.

Mary watched as her father threw the first clod of dirt onto the coffin. Mary was relieved to see that although her father was still crying, the sobbing had ceased. He stepped to where Mary stood, bent down, and kissed her. Then, turning to Eliza, he hugged her also. "I love you both very, very much, but you'll be better off living at your uncle's place. Be good girls for your Uncle Samuel and Aunt Eliza. I'll write you soon." Then he turned away and was assisted by his neighbor toward the waiting buggy at the bottom of the hill.

As the crowd dispersed, Grandma Jane took each girl by the hand and began to walk down the hill. At the foot of the hill, they were greeted by their Uncle Samuel who kissed his mother goodbye and assisted her into the buggy. Then he turned his attention to the girls. "Are you up to riding your pony, Mary, or do you want to ride in the wagon?"

Mary opted for riding her pony so she could ride beside Eliza who had already mounted her pony which was in reality almost a full size horse.

Uncle Samuel continued his directions to the girls. "I'll be riding in front. The two of you will follow. Your Uncle Milton will bring up the rear with the wagon. In about an hour, we should be in Dandridge. We'll stop there for food and to water the horses. I've watered the horses here at your Grandfather Graham's place and have some cool spring water for the two of you. That should do us until we get to Dandridge. Any questions?"

Mary spoke. "Is that where you live, Uncle Samuel? In Dandridge?"

"No, child. When we get to Dandridge, we'll just be getting started good. From there, it's about sixteen or seventeen more miles to where I live. We may stop for the night after about ten more of those miles past Dandridge. We'll see. And remember, if you get tired, you can ride in the wagon. If you think you can't wait an hour before having to use the toilet, you'd better get off your horse and use the one here. There'll be nothing but a bush beside the road before we get to Dandridge." Both Mary and Eliza said they could wait.

With those instructions having been given, the little group started the next leg of the journey. They rode in silence for a while until Mary called out to Eliza, "Are you scared, Eliza? About going to live at Uncle Samuel's house, I mean."

"No, I'm not scared. He seems nice, and maybe it will help us not miss Mama as much, being in a new place."

"Well, I guess that's one way to look at it, Eliza, but I worry about Daddy. He was so sad last night and this morning."

"Mary, you sound like an old person sometime. Daddy will be all right. He has the store to keep him busy. Remember, even yesterday he went to the store."

The girls rode in silence then until they got to Dandridge with Mary continuing to worry about what the preacher had said about her mother "crossing the river" and her daddy being all alone.

In Dandridge, Uncle Samuel found a place for them to eat while the horses rested and had some water. The food was a simple meal but tasty, and Mary was grateful to be off her pony for a while. She'd never before ridden for so long.

While they were eating, Mary asked her Uncle Samuel if it was true that he was a doctor. "Grandma Jane said you went to school in Baltimore and that you're a doctor. What does that mean?"

"That means I see sick people and try to find the right medicine to make them well. Also, sometimes I take care of people who have been injured in some way. At my house, I have an office where I see patients, or if they're too sick to come to the office, I go to people's homes. That keeps me pretty busy, but I'm also planning to open a store and an inn for travelers to spend the night. I live on a busy road where the stage coach comes through and where many people on horseback pass. I'm going to be adding onto our house to provide appropriate accommodations."

Uncle Milton interrupted. "Speaking of space, Samuel, where are you going to put your two charges, and what will Eliza have to say?"

Mary didn't know what "charges" meant, but she thought that Uncle Milton was referring to her and her sister. It dawned on her for the first time that her Aunt Eliza had no idea her household was about to increase in size by two.

Samuel answered his brother. "The girls can have the fourth bedroom upstairs. As for Eliza, I'm sure she will be surprised, but it made sense to me just to bring the girls home with me instead of making another trip. I'm going to be pretty busy overseeing the construction of the addition to the house and stocking the store and won't have time for another trip."

Lunch over, Uncle Samuel got directions to the toilets, and all in the group availed themselves of the facilities before starting the next leg of their journey. At first, both girls resumed the journey riding the horses, but it wasn't too long before Mary called out to Eliza, "My bottom is really getting sore. I think I want to ride in the wagon."

Eliza agreed. "I'm getting sore, too, but I didn't want to be the first to complain."

Mary called out to their Uncle Samuel and asked if she and Eliza could ride in the wagon for a while. All stopped, dismounted, and Mary's pony and Eliza's horse were tied to the back of the wagon. Riding in the wagon was a great relief for the sore bottoms, but did nothing to alleviate the effects of the burning midday sun.

Eliza called out to their Uncle Milton, "How much further will we be traveling today?"

His reply came as a welcome relief to both girls. "We're only about two miles from New Market. We'll stop there, water the horses, and talk it over about where we might spend the night. Samuel said he had an idea about where we might spend the night, and you two don't look up to making it all the way to Samuel's place today."

The last couple of miles to New Market were bumpier than the first five or so from Dandridge, causing the girls to bounce around in the wagon. Mary remarked to Eliza that she almost wished she was back on her pony.

Eliza just laughed and said, "Remember how sore your backside is. Two minutes in the saddle and you'd be begging to get back in the wagon."

Mary rubbed her bottom with one hand and giggled, the first time she'd laughed in three days. "You're right, Eliza. I think I have a permanent imprint of the saddle on my bottom."

Buoyed by the idea of a rest stop in New Market, the girls rode in silence until they began to see a cluster of buildings. "I think we're here," announced

Eliza just as their Uncle Milton called out the same news.

After the little group came to a stop at a place with a watering trough for animals out front, the uncles helped the girls down from the wagon to stretch their legs. They all had a drink of water from the jug they had carried with them from earlier in the day, but the most that could be said for the water was that it was wet.

Mary and Eliza observed their uncles conversing, and then Uncle Samuel walked over to give them the best news they'd heard all day. "We've already ridden sixteen or seventeen miles today. It's almost 4:30 in the afternoon, and you two look like you're about to melt. I know a gentleman who lives about three or four miles from here. If he and his wife can provide us with accommodations, we'll spend the night there and leave the last leg of the trip for tomorrow morning." Then, dipping is big handkerchief in the water, he instructed the girls to bathe their faces and necks.

Continuing on the journey, the girls bounced around in the wagon even more than before because the roads were pretty rough. Neither girl complained though because relief was near.

In thirty minutes or so, Uncle Samuel stopped in front of a house and asked the rest of the group to wait while he went to the door and knocked. They soon saw a man at the door, followed almost immediately by a woman. Following a brief conversation at the door, Samuel motioned to the rest of the party. About the same time, several boys came out of the house, politely said hello, and led the horses off to the barn to care for them.

At the front door, Samuel introduced the hosts as John Nance and his wife Sarah. The man was the first to speak. "It's true my name is John, but everybody calls me Jackie to keep from confusing me with the other John Nance in the community. Please come in. We'll be happy to have you spend the night. The girls look worn out, and all of you will need some food. Helping you folks out is the least we can do to repay the doctor who tended to our son's leg earlier this summer."

At supper, Mary counted the number of people in the host family. There were five boys, the youngest of which appeared to be about her age. Mary thought about eleven children in her grandmother's family. "They must have had a big table," thought Mary.

Mary enjoyed the good food, but by the end of the meal she was so tired she was about to fall over into her plate. Sarah Nance observed that fact and suggested it was time for bed for the girls. She asked two of the older boys to come help her. "Emerson, will you find one of the extra straw ticks and put it on the floor in the bedroom where you and Calvin usually sleep. Find a clean linen sheet and spread it on top of that for the girls. Our gentlemen friends are going to have the bed in that room tonight. You boys can sleep on pallets on the floor in the younger boys' bedroom. No complaints allowed! Calvin, would you pick up the little one who's about to fall asleep in her chair and carry her to bed. The rest of you boys can clear the table while I help the girls get ready for bed. No complaining from you either!"

Sarah Nance motioned for Eliza to follow her, and Calvin scooped up Mary in his arms and followed his mother. Mary barely remembered being picked up by strong arms. She had no memory of Mrs. Nance pulling her dress over her head and leaving her in her petticoat for the night.

After a hardy breakfast the next morning, the rested travelers were ready to be on their way. Mary heard Sarah Nance thanking her Uncle Samuel again for caring for her son's leg earlier in the summer and her uncles thanking the Nance family for their hospitality. Samuel said in parting, "The next doctor's appointment is free. Thank you again for taking us in yesterday evening."

As Mary and Eliza started to mount their animals, they were stopped by their Uncle Samuel who suggested that they just lead their ponies while they took a brief walk to the ferry to cross the river.

Mary's response to hearing they would be crossing a river was immediate. She remembered what her mother had told her about the river, and she remembered what the preacher had said. Grabbing her Uncle Samuel by the hand, Mary blurted out her fears. "Mama always said to stay away from the river. The preacher said yesterday that Mama crossed the river. Then they put the box Mama was in into the ground. I don't want to cross a river."

Seeing the pinched little face and hearing the tremble in Mary's voice, Mary's uncle quickly scooped her up in his arms. "Your mother just meant for you to not play in the river. We're going to be crossing the river on a ferry which is very safe. The man who operates it knows exactly what he's doing. He started helping his dad with it when he was just a boy. Plus, the water is so low right now, with it being August, we could probably just walk across if we didn't mind getting our clothes wet. Now, I'm going to put you down and ask you to lead your pony until we get to the ferry. Then I promise, I'll pick you up and hold you while we cross."

Mary wasn't completely satisfied, but she followed her uncle's directions and led her pony the short distance to the river's edge. Across the river was the ferry with a man and his horse being unloaded. The ferry boat looked to Mary like the floor of a house with no walls or roof .When the ferry operator looked up and saw their little group waiting, he shouted to them, "If you're waiting to cross, I'll be back for you soon."

When the ferry arrived, the operator helped load the animals onto the ferry and secure them to hitching posts. Uncle Samuel picked up Mary as promised and held her while the ferry, held steady by a big cable, glided across the water. Mary hoped her mother's crossing was as smooth.

Safe on the other side of the river, Uncle Samuel sat Mary's feet on the ground and suggested that everyone walk up the slight rise in the road before getting back on their mounts or into the wagon. For the first time, Mary looked up and down the river and thought how pretty it was.

The morning was cooler than the day before, and a slight breeze was blowing. The change in the weather made Uncle Samuel wonder aloud if it was the first hint of fall in the air.

The trip to the Shields' home took less time than Mary expected, but nonetheless, she was glad to hear her uncle announce, "Well, here we are." Before them was a neat white house in a box- like shape Mary had never previously seen.

Uncle Milton spoke up to say he would tend to the animals while Samuel explained their expanded family to his wife. He then helped Mary and Eliza down and suggested they wait in the shade of a tree for their Uncle Samuel's return.

Chapter 3

Sisters and Cousins

The shade of the tree and a slight breeze were a relief to Mary as she and Eliza waited for their Uncle Samuel's return. To pass the time, Mary counted the windows on the front of the house and tried to figure out how many rooms the house contained. Eliza spoke to her once, and Mary lost count and had to start over on her inventory of the windows. By the time she successfully counted the windows, her Uncle Samuel appeared at the front door motioning for the girls to come inside.

As they entered the house, Uncle Samuel welcomed them. "Have a seat here in the parlor. Your Aunt Eliza will be down shortly, and you'll get to meet the rest of the family."

It seemed to Mary like only a few seconds before a pretty young woman with dark hair came down the steps carrying a chubby faced infant who looked at the newcomers warily. "Welcome to our home…your new home. I'm your Aunt Eliza. You probably don't remember me, but you came with your parents to the wedding four years ago when Samuel and I married."

Immediately, Mary's sister Eliza spoke up. "Aunt Eliza, I was seven years old, and I was fascinated because your name was the same as mine, plus I thought you were so pretty. I remember the wedding well."

"I'm pleased to know that you remember the day. It was a special day for me. I guess I've been so busy since then that my memory of your actual age had slipped."

Pausing, the young woman looked up the stairs and called out, "John Howard, are you coming? You need to meet your cousins who are going to be living with us." A creaking sound on the steps could be heard as Aunt Eliza continued. "The baby's name is Mary Jane, but we just call her 'Janie' most of the time."

By this time, Mary could see an impish little face peeking around the corner where the stairs made a turn just before they ended in the room. Mary wasn't sure if the little boy was shy or just playing at making a grand entrance. Mary smiled at the lad, and he, likely realizing he'd been spotted, bounced down the last couple of steps, landing with a thud.

As Aunt Eliza completed the introductions, Uncle Samuel returned from an adjacent room and announced that the noon meal would be ready shortly. "I told Polly that there will be three extra people for the meal. Milton is eating before he starts for home. Polly says there's plenty." Motioning to Mary and Eliza to follow, their uncle continued, "After we've eaten, your Aunt Eliza will show you around the house, and you can get out of those clothes you've worn for two days now. Probably slept in them last night, too, I guess."

Mary looked around now at the room they had entered, recognizing that it was obviously the dining room. The room was furnished with a long table, eight chairs, two high chairs, a side board, and an upright cabinet. The table was covered in a linen cloth, and there were fresh flowers in a vase on the center of the table. Lace curtains hung at the windows which were open, allowing the curtains to sway slightly with the breeze. Plates, silverware, and glasses were already on the table.

Mary could smell the odor of food from the room behind the dining room, and her tummy growling reminded her that it had indeed been a long time since breakfast. As Mary surveyed the room, Uncle Samuel continued. "Come on girls. I'll show you the path to the toilet. Then you can wash up a bit and meet Polly. She's the one who keeps us all fed."

As they entered the kitchen, Mary could see a woman bent over near the fireplace, spooning food into a bowl. Uncle Samuel announced their arrival in the kitchen with "Here they are, Polly. Here are the two new members of our family." Indicating with a pat on first one head and then the other, "Here's Mary, and here's Eliza. Girls, this is Polly."

Mary found herself staring at the most beautiful woman she had ever seen. The woman was tall with straight black hair pulled back and twisted together on the back of her head. She had dark eyes, high cheek bones, and skin the color of coffee that is more cream than coffee. As the beautiful lady spoke, her broad smile revealed very white, straight teeth.

Uncle Samuel spoke again to Polly. "While you get food on the table, I'm going to direct the girls to the path out back and then show them where they can wash the grime off their faces and hands before we sit down to eat." As he spoke, Uncle Samuel led Eliza and Mary to a washstand by the door at the rear of the room. "The outhouse is out this door at the end of the path. When you get back, here's where you can wash."

As he opened the back door for the girls, their uncle spoke again to Polly. "Polly, why don't you set an extra plate on the table and let Sibby join us. She's close to Mary in age, and I'm sure they'll be playmates."

"If you're sure, I'll see to it, sir." Polly paused and waited until Samuel responded with "Absolutely!" Then she called toward an open door on the side of the kitchen. "Sibby, bring the baby with you unless she's asleep, and come in here." Shortly after Mary and Eliza finished washing and made their way back to the dining room, a little girl who looked to be a small version of Polly entered the room. Uncle Samuel directed the child to a seat beside Mary and introduced her with "Girls, this is Sibby, Polly's little girl. After we eat, she can help you unpack your clothes."

Several bowls of food were already on the table. Mary saw that there were pinto beans, slaw, corn, soupy potatoes, sliced tomatoes, and cornbread, all things that she liked. Uncle Samuel asked for those at the table to bow their heads and said a quick blessing before beginning to pass the bowls of food. Polly reappeared and asked what folks wanted to drink.

Aunt Eliza asked Samuel and the girls for details of their trip, and everyone laughed about Mary's sore bottom from riding her pony so far. No mention was made of the fact that the girls' mother had been buried only the morning before. A lot of Aunt Eliza's attention seemed to be focused on getting more food into baby Janie's mouth than spread on her face or dropped on her bib. Little John Howard chatted with his father about whether or not he might get to ride on Mary's pony. His father assured him that he might get to ride on the pony soon, but only with an adult leading the pony around the yard.

Uncle Samuel also shared with his wife his plans to finalize the purchase of their house so he could start the addition of space for a store and medical dispensary and rooms to rent to travelers. "Eliza, I've been thinking while I was on the trip. We've lived here long enough to see that this place is a good fit. There's plenty room enough for the family in the house, and the planned addition will help me provide for the family and serve the community. The nearest store is down the road at Blaine's Crossroads, and more and more travelers are going to be passing on this road. People coming from Knoxville will definitely find this to be a convenient spot to spend the night. The stage coming from the west on Emory Road is already stopping here, but I don't yet have overnight lodging to offer. I think three nice sized rooms will fit above the store, and the entrance to those rooms can be from outside so that travelers don't pass through family quarters. Also, I can use a corner of the store for my medical dispensary so I no longer have to use the dining room for that purpose."

When the meal was complete, Aunt Eliza instructed the girls to take the plates and eating utensils to the kitchen. When they stepped into the kitchen, Mary saw a plump little baby crawling on the floor. The baby crawled as fast as she could to where Sibby stopped with the dishes she was carrying. When Sibby's hands were empty, she reached down, picked up the baby, and announced, "This is my baby sister. Her name is Emmie Lou. I help Mama take care of her."

Polly interrupted. "Sibby, I think I heard Miss Eliza say that you were to help the girls unpack their clothes. Why don't you run and do that now? Emmie Lou can just crawl around in here while I finish with the cleaning up. After you finish helping the young ladies, you can come back and watch Emmie Lou while I go to the garden for vegetables for supper."

Aunt Eliza stuck her head through the kitchen door about that time. "Come on with me, all of you. I want to show Eliza and Mary the rest of the house and then leave them to the unpacking." Mary, Eliza, and Sibby followed Aunt Eliza as she led them back through the dining room and into the parlor. John Howard followed behind.

"As you can see, girls, our downstairs consists of four rooms. You've already seen three of them. The fourth room downstairs is a room next to the kitchen where Polly and her girls live. Upstairs, there are four bedrooms. There is a room for your uncle and me, an adjacent room for the baby, a room for John Howard, and a fourth room which will be yours. Now, be careful going up these stairs. They're narrow on one side where they make a turn. Mr. McDaniel, who built this house thirty years ago, obviously didn't want to waste any space on stairs."

Once up the steps, Aunt Eliza showed Mary and her sister the four rooms, saving their room until last. Their trunk had been brought to their room already, and Aunt Eliza suggested that the girls get started unpacking. "There's a large wardrobe for your clothes that need to be hung up. There's a dresser for the rest. As you unpack, find something you can put on for the rest of the day. Those clothes you're wearing are filthy after two days sweating in the sun. I'm going to see if I can get John Howard and Janie down for naps and may lie down myself for a while. Sibby, when you're finished helping Mary and Eliza, don't forget that your mother expects you back to help her. Girls, you probably think you're too old for a nap, but it wouldn't hurt you to lie down for a rest after your long trip…Welcome to your new home. I'll see you at supper."

As the girls unpacked, they chatted, asking each other a multitude of questions. Sibby had been told by her mother that the girls' mother had died, but she wanted to know why their father had sent them away. Mary and Eliza, in turn, wanted to know why Sibby and her mother were part of the household. In their home, their mother had done all of the cooking. They didn't have someone like Polly who cooked for the family and cleaned up afterward.

When Mary asked whether Sibby and her mother had always lived with their Uncle Samuel and Aunt Eliza, Sibby explained the best she could. "I'm just seven. All I can remember is living with them, but I think we lived with your grandparents first. Anyway, we just moved here earlier this year from Sevier County. Emmie Lou was just a few months old…I can tell you more later, but I'd better go help Mama now.

I'm glad you're here. There haven't been any children I could play with."

With the unpacking completed, Mary and Eliza stripped off their dirty dresses and looked for something else to wear. They noticed a large pitcher and bowl similar to the one they had used downstairs in the kitchen. Closer inspection revealed water already in the pitcher so Eliza suggested that they wash up some more before putting on clean clothes.

After changing into clean garments, Mary remarked to Eliza that she didn't really want to take a nap. "I know Aunt Eliza suggested that we take a nap, but I'm not sleepy."

"I'm not either, but what are we supposed to do with ourselves for the rest of the afternoon? It can't be more than mid-afternoon, can it?"

"Why don't we go downstairs and see what Sibby and her mother are doing? If we were at home, we'd probably be doing chores. Maybe we can help Sibby with her chores."

"That's a good idea. If nobody is going to tell us anything to do other than 'take a nap,' we'll have to figure out for ourselves what to do."

Downstairs everything was quiet. Uncle Samuel was nowhere to be found, and there were no sounds coming from the kitchen as they ventured through the parlor and the dining room. They peeked in the kitchen, which they quickly saw was empty.

"Don't call out for Sibby," Eliza whispered to Mary. "Emmie Lou might be asleep. We don't want to wake her."

At the door to Polly's room, Mary softly whispered, "Sibby, are you there?"

Sibby appeared at the door. "Yes, I'm here. I thought you two were going to take a nap."

"We didn't want to take a nap. At home, we'd be doing chores. Where's your mother?"

"She's out in the garden, picking vegetables for supper."

Mary's face lit with a smile. "That's what we'd be doing at home. Maybe we can help your mother. Is the garden out that door beside the washstand?"

"Yes, it's just a way further than the outhouse. You can't miss it. I have to stay here with Emmie Lou, or I'd go with you."

Without further ado, Mary and Eliza were out the door and headed to the garden.

"Hi, Miss Polly," spoke Mary. "We've come to help."

"Well, what a surprise. Did someone send you?"

"No, Aunt Eliza told us we could take a nap when we were finished unpacking, but we didn't want to nap. At home, we'd be doing chores. We had chores we did every day when we weren't working on our lessons or our needlework."

"Well, what well-mannered and responsible young ladies you are. I can see that your mother taught you well. She'd be proud of you. Doctor Sam told me what happened to your mother. I cried when I heard that. She was like an older sister to me. My mother also died when I was young, and I grew up in the same house as your mother and uncle and their brothers and sisters. Your grandmother Jane was like a mother to me. The family once offered me my freedom papers, but I thought I was better off sticking with the only family I'd ever known."

"Sibby told us that she might have lived with our grandparents at first but was too little to remember living there."

"No, she wasn't much more than a toddler when we moved in with your aunt and uncle, so she's never really known any place else. She's a good girl and helps me with Emmie Lou, but she's been lonely since we moved here in the spring… lonely because there haven't been any other children around. I can tell she's excited that the two of you have come."

Polly paused for a few seconds as she wiped sweat from her face with the bottom of her apron, and then she continued. "So if you really want to help, why don't you pick the vegetables that don't require using a knife. I don't want either of you to cut yourself and get blood all over your clean clothes. I must say you both look a sight better than you did when you first got here today."

Working in separate areas of the large garden, the three picked vegetables in silence until Polly announced that they had all they needed for supper and suggested they carry their baskets into the kitchen. Back in the kitchen, the girls helped Polly unload the vegetables and then washed their hands, chatting all the while to Polly and Sibby, who had emerged from the bedroom lugging Emmie Lou.

Polly gave Emmie Lou some spoons and a pan to play with in a corner of the kitchen the furthest away from the fireplace and suggested that the three girls set the table in preparation for the evening meal. With three working at it, the table was soon set, and the girls trooped back into the kitchen to see if Polly had another assignment for them.

Eliza was the first to ask for more work. "At home, Mama was teaching us to cook. Is there something you'd like us to do?"

Polly's response was a bit of a puzzle to Mary. "Eliza, if you know how to break beans, you can work on that. I'm not going to ask you girls to do more than that in the kitchen until I have directions from your aunt and uncle. Sibby, the baby will be content banging on that pan for a while. Why don't you show Mary where the dust cloths are kept, and the two of you can dust the parlor."

As they dusted in the parlor, Mary and Sibby continued to chat and ask questions of each other about their families and the fact that their mothers had grown up in the same home.

"Sibby, I didn't know our mothers grew up together, did you?"

"No, Mama never talks much about what it was like when she was growing up. I've heard her mention something about eleven children, but I never knew that Doctor Sam was part of the bunch. I didn't know anything about your mother or you and Eliza until today."

"Your mother said she and my mother were like sisters. That makes us like cousins, right?"

Both girls giggled. "I never knew I could have a white cousin, Mary. In fact, if I have cousins of any kind, I don't know about them."

"You're almost as white as me, Sibby, but regardless, you can be my cousin."

The two girls dusted in silence for a few moments until Mary thought of another question to ask her new friend. "Where's your daddy? Did he die?"

"I have no idea. Mama won't talk about it. When I've asked Mama, she says it don't matter who my daddy was. So I don't know if he's dead or alive. I just know Mama was pretty young when I was born, seventeen, I think… I had a step-daddy for a while. He was Emmie Lou's daddy. Mama met him after we moved to Tennessee. They wanted to get married, and Missus Jane helped that happen and even gave a party for them. I was five then, so I remember how much fun it was."

"You said, 'Missus Jane.' That's my grandmother Shields you're talking about, right?"

"Yes, that's what I always call her."

"So, where is your step-daddy now?"

"We don't know for sure, Mary. Mama thinks he was kidnapped. He was on an errand for your granddaddy and just disappeared. Some folks thought he had run away, but Mama said there was no way she would ever believe that. Later, a man who lived down the road a way told your granddaddy that he had met two men on horses and four Negro men in shackles and tied together shuffling down the road, headed south. The men on horseback claimed the men in shackles were runaways being taken back to their owners. The man who told your granddaddy about it said he didn't much believe the men, but there wasn't anything he could do about it because he was unarmed and they had big guns."

"So now, Emmie Lou doesn't have a daddy, you don't have a daddy, and I don't have a mother. That's something else we have in common."

"Mama says that one thing you can count on is life throwing bad things in your path. She also says that when life knocks you down, you just have to pick yourself up and start over."

Chapter 4

"What's My Role?"

At the evening meal, Aunt Eliza asked her nieces for more detail about their trip and what it was like for them to travel so far. Mary made everyone laugh by saying she thought she might still have an imprint of the saddle on her backside. Eliza chimed in with the story of how Mary nearly fell asleep in her plate of food the previous night. "If Mrs. Nance hadn't noticed Mary nodding, she would have planted her face in her plate. At that point, she had to be carried upstairs to bed by the oldest son, and Mrs. Nance had to pull her dress off for her."

"Well, you don't look that tired tonight, even though I heard rumors that you found a nap unnecessary this afternoon. I wish I had that much energy."

"Are you upset that we didn't take a nap, Aunt Eliza?"

"Oh, goodness no! It's just that I HAVE to have a nap every afternoon. I suppose I think everybody else needs one also. I'm glad that you've bounced back from the rigors of the trip."

At the end of the meal, Eliza and Mary carried all the plates to the kitchen and said good-night to Polly and Sibby. They declined Aunt Eliza's offer of helping them prepare for bed, saying they believed they could handle that by themselves just fine. They need no encouragement however to take advantage of the offer of an early bedtime.

Once Eliza and Mary got into their nightclothes and crawled into bed, conversation was brief. "Eliza, this feels pretty comfy. Last night we were on pallets on the floor."

Eliza laughed and quickly responded. "I'm surprised you remember anything about the pallet after having to be carried to bed."

"You just had to tell that story, didn't you?"

"It was too funny not to tell, and that boy who carried you was so nice looking, I thought I might try falling into my plate also."

By the time Eliza finished speaking, Mary was asleep. In a half minute more, Eliza followed suite.

When Eliza and Mary ventured downstairs the following morning, there was nobody in the dining room yet, so they went into the kitchen to speak to Polly and see if Sibby was up. Mary spoke first. "Where is everybody?"

"I think they'll be down shortly. Your uncle was just through here a few minutes ago. He had John Howard with him, taking him out to potty. You need to do the same and then wash up for breakfast."

By the time the girls had followed Polly's suggestion, Uncle Samuel and John Howard were seated at the table. Little Janie was on her daddy's knee. Polly was making trips back and forth, bringing biscuits, eggs, sausage, and gravy. Milk had been poured for the children, and there were slices of cantaloupe in a big bowl. Aunt Eliza's seat was empty.

Uncle Samuel was quick to make an explanation about his wife's absence. "Your aunt isn't feeling well this morning, so she won't be joining us."

As the meal progressed, it was evident that Uncle Samuel was not accustomed to eating while also trying to give a baby a few bites and simultaneously trying to keep her hands out of the plate. The amusing scene prompted giggles from Eliza and Mary.

Polly came to the dining room to offer more coffee and observed the source of the giggles. "Give me the baby. I'll feed her in the kitchen and let you eat in peace."

"Thank you, Polly. I believe I'll take you up on that offer."

With peace returned to the table, Eliza broached the topic of expected roles in their new home. "Uncle Samuel, Mary and I had specific things we were responsible for at home. We had chores, we had lessons, and we were learning how to cook. I know we just got here, but what are we going to be doing every day?"

"Eliza, I'm sorry I haven't had time to think about that much. I did promise your father that you would be provided with an education. You will not be treated as servants, but you will be expected to help with chores like any family member. If you want to help Polly some with the same kind of chores you did at home, that will be fine. I'll speak to her about that. Also, I suspect that my wife is going to need some help with John Howard. You can take him out in the backyard to play, but be sure to keep him out of the front yard and away from the road. He's curious about everything and can run really fast. I'll speak to my wife when she's feeling better, and we'll see if we can work out a bit of a schedule for you."

"Thank you, Uncle Samuel; that helps."

"It may be a while before I can arrange for a teacher for you. I'm going to have my hands full overseeing the construction of the addition to the house, but I won't forget the promise I made to your father."

Hearing all of this, Mary had her own question. "Uncle Samuel, do you think we're always going to live here?"

"For the foreseeable future, yes. Your father is busy full time with the store, and since he doesn't believe in owning slaves, it is doubtful there would be anyone to take care of the household except you two. I know you're big girls, mature for your age, and very responsible, but that would be an untenable situation. So, yes, you should consider this home to be your home. We welcome you, we love you, and I hope the next several years of your life will be happy ones. .. Oh, and today, would you play with John Howard and try to keep him entertained since his mother isn't feeling well. While he takes a nap this afternoon, you can do as you please with your time. You can play with Sibby if she isn't helping her mother or help her with her chores… just whatever you want to do. Polly or Sibby will let you know when it's time for lunch. I have some business to which I must attend but should be home for supper."

With their uncle readying to leave, Eliza and Mary headed to the kitchen, along with John Howard, who was still talking about Mary's pony. In the kitchen, they found both Janie and Emmie Lou pulled up to the work table feeding themselves from tin pans.

Polly laughed when the girls came into the room and gestured toward the babies. "Missus Eliza thinks this baby won't eat if she doesn't spoon food into her. As you can see, she's eating just fine and making no more mess than when someone else is feeding her. You two run along with John Howard. I heard what Doctor Sam told you. When the baby is through eating, I'll clean her up and take her upstairs and check on Missus Eliza."

By lunch time, Aunt Eliza was feeling well enough to be at the table and eat a light lunch. Polly took baby Janie to the kitchen again for the meal. Afterward, she returned the baby to her upstairs room and put both the baby and John Howard down for their naps. Eliza announced she was going to go upstairs and examine the books on the bookshelf in their room to see if she could find one to read. Mary chose to stay and visit with Polly and Sibby.

"Polly, I miss my Mama so much."

"Of course you do, honey. It's just been four or five days since she died. Come here and give me a hug."

Polly sat down in a kitchen chair and pulled Mary onto her lap and hugged her tight while the tears flowed.

"You cry all you want to, honey. There's nothing more important to me right now than wiping your tears."

"Did you cry a lot when your Mama died?"

"I sure did, and your grandmother Jane hugged me on her lap and dried my tears many times. Don't you ever forget that I have a lap and my apron can soak up a bunch of tears."

"I love you, Polly. Can I call you 'Aunt Polly'?"

"Run that idea by your uncle. If it's alright with him, I'd be honored to be called Aunt Polly."

Polly and Mary sat in silence for a few more minutes before Polly suggested that Mary go see what Sibby was doing. "If Emmie Lou is asleep, the two of you can go out and play. I'll hear Emmie Lou when she wakes up."

By supper time, Uncle Samuel had returned. During the meal, he inquired about how the day had gone. After hearing a report from Eliza and Mary, he said "Sounds like that went well. Consider that your plan for the day until I get a teacher for you. You can play with John Howard in the morning, but the afternoons are yours to do with as you please. You can read, do needlework, play, or help Polly with chores. Keep practicing your penmanship, too, and show your aunt what you've done. I'm afraid my penmanship is not refined enough to make me a good judge."

As suggested by their uncle, the next several days followed pretty much the same pattern as the first day for Mary and Eliza. Their aunt was absent from breakfast every morning but seemed better by noon. The girls played with John Howard in the morning and did as they pleased in the afternoon. Sometimes, they took turns reading aloud to John Howard until he fell asleep for his afternoon nap. After that, they read, did needlework, or helped Polly and Sibby with chores.

Frequently, Eliza continued to read while Mary played with Sibby.

When construction got underway on the addition to the house, naps became hard to come by for everyone. The near constant sounds of hammering outweighed almost any level of sleepiness. Only baby Janie seemed to nap in spite of the loud noise.

Construction to the house also made it difficult to provide outdoor playtime for John Howard. As his daddy had said, he was curious about everything and could run very fast. When he was playing outside, it took both Eliza and Mary to keep him corralled, away from the construction and the front yard.

As weeks passed and fall weather began to be downright chilly, Aunt Eliza asked to do a clothes inventory with the girls. "Cold weather is coming, and I need to see what clothing you have that is suitable for winter. Mary, you may be able to wear some things that your sister wore last year. We'll have to see about that. Some of your things might be passed to Sibby. Whatever each of you lack needs to be determined now because a couple of seamstresses will be employed for the next several weeks to make garments for all family members. Eliza, you are getting so tall that you may be able to wear some of my dresses that I don't fit into any more."

Later, Eliza confided to Mary that their aunt had remarked to her that it was obvious she was "becoming a woman, body-wise," and had asked her what their mother had told her about changes she should expect in her body. "I told her that Mama had explained everything to both of us and that we knew about body changes and babies and everything. I told her how we even watched kittens being born. Then she told me that she's expecting another baby."

"I know."

"How did you know? Did she tell you, too?"

"No, Sibby told me. Her mother had told her, but she said not to tell."

"Well, you could have told me."

"It doesn't really matter now, does it? Aunt Eliza told you herself. So don't get in a huff."

Silence ensued then, but as time went on, Eliza seemed to spend more and more time with her aunt, and Mary increasingly spent her free time playing with Sibby.

During their playtime one day, Mary asked Sibby if she would always be her friend. "You're my best friend, actually my only friend, Sibby, except for my sister. Will you promise to always be my friend?"

"Sure, I'll always be your friend, Mary."

"When we're grown up, will you live close to me?"

"I'll always be your friend, Mary, but I might not be able to live close to you unless you buy me."

"What do you mean, buy you? You don't buy friends."

"You don't know nothin, do you, Mary? Your uncle owns my mother. That means he owns me, too."

"No, I guess I don't know 'nothin,' as you say. I don't know how you own another person."

"You remember Mama talking about 'freedom papers' and me telling you about my stepdaddy? And who do you think those folks are who live in the cabins behind the garden? Your uncle is good to them, but they are slaves. That is what folks are called when someone else has papers saying they're property."

"Property? Like a farm or a store or something? Well then, I guess I'll have to buy you and give you your freedom papers."

"That's sweet, Mary, but regardless, I will always be your friend and your secret cousin…Right?"

"Right!"

It was near that same time that Mary discovered that Sibby didn't know how to read. She was practicing her penmanship when Sibby asked what all those symbols meant. Mary was shocked. She had assumed that all children were taught how to read.

"You don't know your ABCs? That's what those symbols mean, and together they make words. Does your mother know how to read?"

"I think she does, at least a little, but she said a lot of people don't think slaves should know how to read."

"Well, I think that's nonsense. I'll teach you how to read, and that can be another secret we share. I'll be teaching you while I'm practicing my penmanship and while I'm reading to John Howard."

Mary began her lessons with Sibby by showing her how all the letters looked in both printed and written form. Next, she showed Sibby how to write her own name. It was then that she learned that her friend's name wasn't really Sibby.

"My name isn't really Sibby. Mama named me Sylvia, but I couldn't say that when I was little. I called myself 'Sibby,' and that name just stuck."

"Well, I'll teach you how to write both names, but you'll always be Sibby to me."

As fall progressed and Christmas neared, Mary's lessons with Sibby continued, usually under the guise of practicing her own penmanship or while reading to John Howard. She even asked if she could teach needlework to Sibby, and nobody seemed to take issue with Sibby stitching letters and numbers on a piece of linen.

Aunt Eliza sometimes listened to Mary and Eliza reading to John Howard and occasionally inspected their penmanship and needlework. She often praised the girls on their progress and told their uncle that the girls were doing quite well, education wise, even without a hired teacher.

A new normal settled into the household with construction on the addition complete. Uncle Samuel was busy stocking the store and setting up his medical office in one front corner. The store would carry everything from fine saddles to calico, linen, and silk. Furniture had been purchased and placed in the rooms for travelers upstairs. Uncle Samuel said the store and inn would open immediately after Christmas.

Christmas celebration started on Christmas Eve with the hanging of stockings. The next morning the family gathered early to open gifts. Both Mary and Eliza received several new dresses, petticoats, shoes, and stockings, and new books shipped from Baltimore. Their stockings were filled with candy and nuts.

William Graham had sent small decorated wooden boxes for his daughters and wooden toys for the Shields children. Notes inside the boxes expressed his love and deep regret at not being able to spend Christmas with his "precious little girls." Mary almost cried when she read her note, not only because she missed her father but also because the thought of him being all alone just broke her heart. "Oh, how I wish I could give Daddy a hug" was all she could manage to say when her Aunt Eliza asked her about her gift.

Mary gave her sister a handkerchief she had embroidered with an E on one corner. For Sibby, she had made a doll dress for her rag doll.

After gifts were exchanged among the family members, Mary went to give Sibby her gift. She was happy to see that a stocking had been provided for Sibby also. As Sibby dressed her doll in the new dress, Mary showed the little box her father had made to Polly and told her about the note. Then, the tears, held back earlier, began to flow. "Oh, Aunt Polly, I miss my

Daddy so much, and all I can think of right now is him all alone. He must be so sad. I think of him often, the way he was the day Mama died and especially the day she was buried."

As Mary sat on Polly's lap and had her tears wiped with what Polly had come to call her "magic apron," she slowly gained control and ceased to cry.

"Aunt Polly, do you think my Daddy knows how much I love him?"

"Oh, I think he does, but why don't you write him a letter and tell him so? I bet he'll be pleased to see how pretty your penmanship is now, and you can tell him how your Aunt Eliza listens to you read and about your new books. See, I know about them; I helped unpack them. I also know about the little secret you and Sibby have, but it's safe with me."

"Oh, Aunt Polly, I do love you. I still miss my Mama, but it's almost like I have two mamas now…you and Aunt Eliza."

"You are one precious child, Mary Graham. My daughter couldn't have a better friend and playmate than you. Now give me one more hug and then go see if Sibby has her doll dressed in her new dress. I have a Christmas dinner to prepare."

Shields Station store and inn did open immediately after Christmas, and two young men were hired to assist in the store, keep the rooms upstairs clean and ready for guests, and make trips to Knoxville to purchase supplies for the store. One of the rooms upstairs was designated as their sleeping quarters. The young men were welcome to take meals with the family, but guests were not. Uncle Samuel said the only exception would be if somebody really important, like President Jackson, stopped for the night. Most guests would have to settle for simple meals in the tavern in the rear of the store.

The store was accessible from the main part of the house, but the rooms in the inn were separate. A stairway at the rear of the store led to a hallway in the inn quarters upstairs, but the door leading to those stairs was locked after the tavern closed for the night. Guests who needed to avail themselves of the toilet during the night had to use the outside stairs. Samuel

Shields had no intention of placing his family at risk from any unscrupulous overnight guest.

Samuel Shields may have though his life would settle down after construction of the store and inn were complete, but to Mary it seemed he was busier than ever. He was always tending to the store, seeing sick people, or patching up folks with injuries. Only occasionally did he have time to ask Mary and Eliza about their studies in the new books or what they had learned recently. No more mention was made about a teacher, and Mary surmised that her uncle must think she and Eliza were learning just fine with only a little assistance from their Aunt Eliza.

One of the biggest differences as winter progressed was that Aunt Eliza was increasingly dependent on Mary and her sister to chase after little Janie. Janie's legs were short, but she was more than her pregnant mother could keep up with. So Eliza and Mary now had both John Howard and little Janie in their care for large portions of the day.

In the spring, Aunt Eliza gave birth to another baby girl. This child was named Eliza, but was called

Lizzie from the beginning. When Mary and her sister learned what the baby was to be called, both expressed relief that there was not going to be yet another person in the house actually called Eliza. Young Eliza was especially adamant about the name, telling Mary, "If they had said they were going to call the baby Eliza, I think I would have had to change my name. And for heaven's sake, if you ever have a baby, don't name it Eliza. Think of something different."

Polly was asked if she would like to be nanny to the children instead of cook. She thought it over for a few days before saying she'd rather feed all members of the household rather than chase after children all day.

Mary and Eliza still played with the children a lot, but a nanny was found to carry the major responsibility for childcare.

Chapter 5

Proposals

For a long time, Mary fanaticized that her father would come get her and her sister and take them back to live with him, but weeks turned into months and months into years, and slowly that dream faded. She resigned herself to the fact that she would be continuing to live with her uncle and aunt.

Meanwhile, Samuel Shields' dream of a prosperous store and inn came to fruition. Business flourished, and even President Jackson stayed at the inn on his way from Nashville to Washington.

Just as the business grew, so did the size of the Shields family with Annie born to Aunt Eliza in 1835 and Lon born in 1837. Polly confessed to Eliza Shields that she believed she had made the right decision four years previously when she opted to stick with cooking for the family instead of "herding the flock." Eliza Shields could only laugh and tell Polly she was undoubtedly right.

Another major change to the Shields' household occurred in 1837 with the marriage of Mary's sister Eliza at age sixteen. In May, Mary and her sister were invited by their Uncle Milton and Aunt Priscilla to come for a two week visit at their home in Morristown. Aunt Priscilla said she thought the girls needed the opportunity to meet and socialize with young people near their age. The trip sounded like great fun to both girls, and they eagerly prepared for the venture.

Soon after Mary and Eliza's arrival at Morristown, Aunt Priscilla announced that she had planned a party for their benefit. On the day of the party, tables were set up on the lawn and covered with white linen cloths. Mary and Eliza helped their aunt arrange bouquets of roses for the tables and carry the best china to the tables. Ample amounts of food were prepared, including an entire pig roasted in the yard by one of Uncle Milton's employees.

A large crowd of prominent people had been invited to the party, and Mary thought it looked like half the people in town. All the ladies were dressed in what appeared to be their best dresses, and the gentlemen were equally well clad. Dining was buffet style, and people were free to mingle and chat. A trio of musicians played on the nearby porch with the music mingling with the chatter of the guests. Mary thought she could never have imagined such a lovely scene.

When the evening was finally over and the girls had retired to their room, Eliza was flushed with excitement. "Did you see the handsome young man I talked with for so long?"

"Yes, you did seem to be monopolizing his time."

"Maybe it was the reverse, Mary. In fact, he's coming back to see me tomorrow afternoon."

"What's his name? I met so many people today that I can't remember even half their names."

"His name is Frank Taylor. How do you think the name Eliza Taylor sounds?"

"That's a bit premature, isn't it? You only met him today."

"Well, I'm entitled to dream, aren't I?"

"Well, dream on, sister; I'm going to bed."

The young man did come back to see Eliza the following day and most of the remaining days of the two week visit. One the last day of the visit, Eliza announced that her beau was going to accompany them and their Uncle Milton on the return trip to Shields Station and ask their Uncle Samuel if he might have a job for him. Mary began to think that her sister's fantasy of becoming Eliza Graham Taylor wasn't too farfetched.

Doctor Shields did find a job for young Frank, asking him to handle the operation of the store while he oversaw the construction of another addition to the house. This arrangement allowed Eliza and Frank to have daily contact for the entire summer.

Near the end of the summer, Eliza announced first to Mary and then to her uncle and aunt that Frank had proposed marriage and she had accepted. Mary's response was mixed. "I know this is what you've wanted, Eliza, but you are only sixteen."

"So?"

"Sixteen is awfully young, Elia. If you marry this young, you'll probably wind up with a dozen kids."

"Well, our mother was one of eleven, wasn't she, and if I remember correctly, our daddy was one of ten children. So, I guess I'd just be carrying on a family tradition."

"Have you told Uncle Sam and Aunt Eliza?"

"No, we plan to tell them after dinner tonight and ask their blessing."

"They'll surely say yes, although they might ask Frank to ride over to Graham's Chapel and ask Daddy."

"Could be, but seems to me that Daddy pretty much completely turned all responsibility for us over to Uncle Sam."

"Do I get to be in your wedding?"

"Do you think you're old enough?"

"If you can get married at sixteen, I'm old enough at thirteen to be in your wedding."

"I'm just teasing you, Mary. Of course you'll be in my wedding, and I may name one of my dozen kids after you."

Uncle Samuel and Aunt Eliza did give their blessing, and notice of the upcoming nuptials was sent to William Graham. In spite of having a new baby to attend to, Aunt Eliza quickly helped plan the wedding and sent Frank to make arrangements with the minister. On the selected date, Frank's parents came as did William Graham. The ceremony took place in the new parlor with Mary standing by her sister as her only attendant. Refreshments prepared by Polly were served in the dining room before the young couple left for their new home in Morristown.

After all the festivities had ended, Mary had a chance to spend some time with her father. "I'm glad you came, Daddy. I didn't know if you would be able to make it or not, and when you didn't arrive until just before time for the wedding I was really afraid you hadn't been able to get away."

"I had to come see the oldest of my two little girls get married."

"I still miss you, Daddy, and I worry about you."

"I'm alright, Mary. You shouldn't worry about me."

"Do you still live in the store instead of the house, Daddy?"

"I'm afraid so, honey. I've never been able to move back to the house. It's like the house has no soul without your mother in it."

"Oh, Daddy, that's so sad."

"Please don't be sad. I am alright. Living in the store is just my way of dealing with what life has given me."

"Well, if you say so, but I'm not totally convinced."

"Convinced or not, I just want to spend the rest of my time here enjoying being with you. You've changed even more than your sister since I last saw you. I suppose you'll be getting married too before I hardly know it."

"Well, I promise you this, Daddy. I'm not getting married at sixteen. Now, come on; I want you to meet my best friend, Sibby. She's probably in the kitchen helping her mother."

After breakfast the next morning, William Graham kissed Mary goodbye and mounted his horse for the long ride home.

After Eliza's marriage, Mary concentrated on helping John Howard, now eight years old, and Janie, age six, with their reading. A teacher had been hired when John Howard was five, only to discover that the lad could already read quite well, courtesy of his older cousins. However, the teacher did supplant a large portion of the teaching that Mary and her sister had provided.

With both a teacher and a nanny on the scene, more often than not, Mary helped Polly and Sibby with household chores or assisted Aunt Eliza with the youngest of the five children, infant Lon. Sometimes she gave the nanny a break from chasing after four year old Lizzie and two year old Annie. If there was nothing else to do, Mary would find her way to her uncle's library and study some of his medical books, having already read pretty much everything else in the house.

Based on the spacing of the other Shields' children Mary expected there would be another infant added to the household when Lon was two, but that didn't happen. Mary couldn't help but be somewhat disappointed that there wasn't going to be another small baby in need of attention, but after thinking it over, she had to admit that Aunt Eliza probably deserved a break after having five children in the first nine years of her marriage.

With no new infant to assist with, Mary asked her uncle if she could help in the store. After much wheedling from Mary, her Uncle Samuel finally agreed that she could assist in the store under select circumstances.

"When I'm in the store, you can help with stocking and sales during daytime hours. You will not assist during evening hours when travelers may be dining or imbibing spirits in the rear of the store. Do you understand?"

"That sounds reasonable to me. I just want something to do besides helping with household chores and helping the nanny."

Soon after that exchange, Mary did start helping in the store. Meeting new people was a pleasure she had not anticipated but found to be one of her most favorite things about the new endeavor. In early summer of her seventeenth year, Mary was working in the store with her uncle when a tall, dark- haired, and very nice looking young man came into the store. Although Mary didn't recognize him, her uncle obviously knew him well.

"Cal, how are you, and how are your parents? I haven't seen your dad in a while."

"I'm fine, and my parents are fine. Dad just sends me on a lot of errands while he concentrates on the farm."

"Mary, do you remember Cal Nance?"

"No, I don't believe I do."

"Well, that's no wonder. Likely the only time you met was when you were eight years old and we stopped at his parents' home after traveling all day from Graham's Chapel. You were so tired you nearly fell asleep in your plate of food."

Cal flashed a smile at Mary. "I remember that day. I thought you were the bravest little girl. Your mother had just been buried that morning, and you had traveled all day on your pony or in the wagon in the blazing hot sun, but you didn't make one complaint."

"I was probably too tired to complain."

"Somehow I doubt that. Anyway, you impressed me. I remember that I thought as I carried you upstairs that you were very special. Now I can see that you're still very special."

Mary didn't quite know how to respond to the last part of Cal's comment so she just asked if she could help the young man find anything. When he declined assistance, Mary resumed stocking the shelves. When the young man finished shopping, Doctor Sam tallied up the order and accepted payment. As he left the store, Cal looked directly at Mary, waved, and said, "See you soon."

Mary was intrigued with the fact that the young man remembered her from when she was eight years old. She tried to think back to that night almost nine years in the past. She had vague memories of counting the boys at the table and noting that there were five of them ranging from a couple who looked grown down to one who appeared to be about her age. The young man who had just left the store had mentioned that he was the one who carried Mary upstairs, so he must have been one of the older boys. Mary smiled to herself, remembering his "See you soon" comment. She hoped that he would keep that promise.

Cal Nance did keep that promise. In fact, he returned within a week, saying he had forgotten some things on his previous trip. After gathering up a few things to purchase, he lingered, chatting with Mary for several minutes. The next week, he repeated the same thing. After observing Cal's behavior, Mary's Uncle Sam remarked "I believe that boy is getting mighty forgetful" and winked at Mary.

Within a month of that first meeting between Cal and Mary, Cal asked for permission to visit the home specifically to see Mary, and Doctor Sam was quick to grant permission. Mary's uncle teased her about the request, saying he supposed Cal thought his only other option was to buy everything in the store to satisfy his desire to have time with Mary.

After that, Cal did visit often. Sometimes he was invited for a meal. Other times he and Mary spent time alone in the parlor or on the big back porch that was part of the addition to the house. On one day in mid-July. Mary and Cal were escaping the midday heat in the big parlor when Mary recounted the story of what her father had said about his house having "no soul" after the death of his wife.

Immediately Cal remarked, "I think I understand that, Mary, and I need you to be the soul of my house. Will you marry me? I'm to the point I can hardly stand to leave you when I have to say goodbye and go home. I love you, Mary Graham."

Mary didn't hesitate. "I love you, too, Calvin Nance, and I will be happy to be your wife."

"Oh, that's a relief. I've been trying to find the perfect time to ask you. I tried to figure out something really romantic to say, but just now I couldn't help myself. I just blurted it out."

"I think you were very romantic, planned or not, but I would prefer to wait until next spring to marry. Aunt Eliza is expecting another baby, and I would like to be here to help her for a little while after the baby is born. She has done so much for me in the last nine years."

"That's perfect, Mary, although I'd like to carry you off today. Dad gave me sizeable acreage when I turned twenty-one, and I want to build a nice house for you. I'll get started on the construction right away. By starting now, I think we can get the house under roof before the fall rains, and we can finish the inside over the winter."

"It sounds like you've been planning this for a while."

"Yes, I suppose I have, but I was just hesitant to propose for fear you'd say no."

"Well, now that I've said yes, tell me about this house you're about to start building."

"Better than that, Mary, I'll draw the floor plan for you to see so you can make changes if you wish. What I've planned is an L-shaped eight room house plus a free standing kitchen. Downstairs, there will be a parlor and a library/sitting room on the front of the house separated by a wide hall and a stairway leading to the upper level. The long side of the L will have a second entrance beyond the library and then a bedroom and the dining room. The downstairs bedroom will have a small stairway leading upstairs to a small hallway separating the far bedroom from the bedroom which will be ours. Our bedroom and the remaining two will open onto the hallway to which the front steps will lead. Two bonuses I haven't mentioned are the inclusion of a closet in our bedroom and a small room adjoining our room which will be large enough for a crib. That small room will also open into the bedroom next to it. The freestanding kitchen will be across from the back porch and the entry to the dining room. Having the kitchen separate keeps heat out of the house in the summer and also is safer in case of a fire."

"Maybe that will all make more sense when I see the actual floorplan. It sounds like a lot of house."

"Well, I have been thinking about this for a while. You didn't ask me how I can afford this much house, but I'll tell you anyway. I've been raising crops and animals for sale ever since Dad gave me the land, and I've done quite well."

"I wasn't going to ask that, but the house sounds perfect. I think you've told me everything except where our home is to be."

"Do you remember where you crossed the river on the ferry just after leaving my parents' home nine years ago? There is a bluff overlooking the river near the ferry crossing. That's where our house will be built. The side of the house will face the river so there will be a view of the river from three of the bedrooms upstairs, including ours. A lane will lead past the side of the house toward the barn and other farm buildings."

"The house will be on this side of the river, right? And we don't have to cross the ferry to get there?"

"No, we don't have to cross the river to get there, but why would that be a problem? The ferry is safe. It's operated by my cousins."

"It's just a thing I have about rivers. I'll try to explain it to you sometime. Right now, we need to go share our news with my uncle and aunt."

Chapter 6

Mixed Emotions

On the day after the engagement announcement to the family, Aunt Eliza remarked to Mary, "You realize you're marrying one of the most eligible bachelors in the county, don't you? Half the girls in the county would give anything to be in your shoes."

"I didn't know it was a contest, Aunt Eliza. It just happened. The first time he flashed that smile and looked at me with those grey-green eyes, I was smitten. And for some reason, he seems to think I'm special."

"You are special, my dear, and I think you're going to have a wonderful marriage."

"Did you know Cal has already planned a house for us and intends to get started on the construction right away? He has it planned down to every detail. He said I could make changes if I wanted to, but I think it sounds perfect in every way, even to the site he's selected overlooking the river. The house will have a parlor, a library, a dining room, five bedrooms, one of which will be downstairs, and a freestanding kitchen. Cal even says there's a small bonus room big enough for a crib next to the bedroom that will be ours."

"When does he expect the house to be ready?"

"He wants to get it under roof before fall rains and then finish the inside over the winter. I told him that sounds perfect because I wanted to be here for a while after the baby arrives to help you what I can."

"That's sweet of you, Mary, but I could manage if you want to marry sooner. I had my first two before you were a member of this household and the next two before you were old enough to be of much help, and this will be my sixth baby."

"Do you think this baby will be born sometime after Christmas?"

"That's what Samuel thinks, but I do seem to be getting bigger earlier in my pregnancy than with my other babies. Maybe we'll have a Christmas baby."

"Well, whenever you have the baby, I plan to be here to help, Aunt Eliza."

"Enough baby talk! Let's start planning your wedding."

Excitement filled the air in the days that followed. Aunt Eliza seemed almost as excited about Mary's engagement as though it were her own. Suggestions were made about guest lists, attire, food, and even when spring flowers such as roses would be in bloom.

Then an event occurred in late July which seemed to Mary like the worst thing that had happened since the death of her mother. The day had been oppressively hot, especially in the kitchen. Emmie Lou told her mother that she was going outside to sit on the back steps and cool off for a while.

Polly, focused on cleaning up the kitchen, thought nothing of it and said, "Sure."

Minutes passed, Polly was busy and not really thinking about how long Emmie Lou had been outside. When she noticed that it was now dark, she asked Sibby to check on her sister.

Sibby soon returned to say that there was no sign of Emmie Lou. She had even called her name several times without response.

Polly was alarmed. "Go find Doctor Sam. Tell him that Emmie Lou has disappeared from the back steps and we have no idea where she is."

Knowing that Samuel Shields often oversaw the closing of the tavern in the rear of the store, Sibby went to the store first.

When Samuel Shields heard of Emmie Lou's disappearance, he turned to Luke, one of the boys employed to assist with the store and inn, and immediately instructed him to bolt the door leading to the rooms upstairs. "We only have one guest tonight, correct?"

"Yes, that's correct, sir."

Turning to the other employee, Doctor Sam barked instructions as he opened a locked cabinet in his medical dispensary and took out two rifles and a pistol, "Come with me, boys. We're going on a little hunting expedition." On the way out of the store, he grabbed two lengths of rope.

The three men exited the store and quickly made their way to the rear steps leading to the rooms in the inn. On the way, Doctor Sam confirmed the room to which the guest had been assigned. With pistol drawn and without knocking, he burst into the room, his two employees right behind him.

There on the bed was Emmie Lou, naked and crying, with the guest naked except for his shirt. Doctor Sam's rage was immediate.

"I ought to shoot you right now, you worthless piece of scum, or take you out back to Oscar and big Ned and tell them what you've done. There might not be enough left of you to bury after they finish with you. But that can wait until morning while I decide whether to give you over to them or let the sheriff handle the matter. Right now, we're just going to tie you up and lock you in this room overnight."

The guest/prisoner tried to protest. "I don't know why you're making such a fuss. She's just a little nig…," but Doctor Sam interrupted.

"Don't you dare call this child what you were about to call her. She is a treasured member of this household. I heard you bragging downstairs earlier tonight about how your daddy is some kind of big judge up in Virginia. Let's see him get you out of this!"

As he scooped up Emmie Lou in a sheet and started to exit the room, Doctor Sam gave one other instruction. "Once this scum is tied up and locked in this room, one of you needs to stay outside the room through half the night. Then you can wake the other one and let him take over. I'll check on things downstairs after I get Emmie Lou taken care of. Probably, there's nothing in the store or tavern that can't wait until morning for your attention."

Then he carried Emmie Lou down the steps and in the backdoor to the kitchen where a worried Polly was pacing the floor. Once Emmie Lou was in her mother's arms, Doctor Sam asked her, "Did the man hurt you?"

The answer, through tears, was "yes."

"Are you still hurting?"

Emmie Lou answered, "Some."

Turning to Polly, Doctor Sam instructed her to give Emmie Lou a bath and let him know in the morning if she was still hurting. "If she's still hurting, I can examine her then if you want. I think she's been through enough trauma tonight and don't want to do anything to cause her any more distress…and Emmie Lou, please remember that you did not do anything wrong, and the man who hurt you will be punished!"

When Samuel Shields finally got to his own bedroom, he told Eliza that he had never come so close to killing a man as he had that night. Eliza was equally horrified to hear about the night's events.

Early the next morning, the problem of what to do with the rapist was solved. A small posse had tracked him from Knoxville where he had committed an equally heinous crime. The men in the posse had spotted the criminal's horse tied up out front. They appeared to love finding him trussed up like a roasted turkey, bare butt shining. One laughed and said to the other two men in the posse "It's a shame we can't haul him in exactly like this."

In the days that followed, Polly, Sibby, and Mary all doted on Emmie Lou, and with the resilience that only a child can show, she appeared to be recovering remarkably well from her ordeal. It wasn't until several weeks had passed that the adults began to suspect that Emmie Lou's ordeal was far from over. Polly was the first to observe suspicious signs: morning nausea, afternoon sleepiness, and breast enlargement. She shared her concerns with Doctor Sam and said, based on her observations, that she was afraid that Emmie Lou was pregnant. Doctor Sam agreed that the early signs of pregnancy were present but declined to examine Emmie Lou, telling Polly, "If she is pregnant, we'll know soon enough. I pray she isn't. She's barely eleven years old, but if she is pregnant, I'll do everything I can to help her through it. Do you think she suspects?"

"Not yet, but if I notice any more changes, I'll ask her what she thinks is causing her body to change. We'll take it from there."

"You are a wise woman, Polly. A lot of doctors could learn a thing or two from you."

Right after the assault on Emmie Lou, Mary shared with Cal what had happened. The terms he used to describe the perpetrator were pretty much the same as those words used by Doctor Sam on the night of the attack. Then his concern focused on Mary. "That just makes me more anxious to get you away from here and into our own home. I know your uncle runs a high-class establishment and is noted for having one of the nicest stage coach stations in these parts, but there's just too much travel on this road and too many unsavory characters passing through. I want you where I can keep you safe."

Weeks passed and as the leaves began to fall, it was readily apparent that Emmie Lou was pregnant. Polly followed through with her plan to ask her daughter if she knew what was happening to her body. Emmie Lou's response came as a complete shock to Polly.

"I think the changes to my body mean I'm going to have a baby. That man did something bad to me, but I'm going to be compensated – that's a word Mary taught me – by having a baby."

Polly couldn't think of a thing to say except "God bless you, child," as she hugged Emmie Lou close before she could see the tears in her mother's eyes.

As Christmas approached, Cal kept Mary apprised of progress on their house. Construction was proceeding as planned, so despite her worries about Emmie Lou's pregnancy, Mary tried to focus on the fact that in six months she would be moving into her new home with Cal.

Aunt Eliza's pregnancy seemed to be progressing normally, but she complained that she felt enormous this time. Mary didn't say so, but she pretty much agreed that Aunt Eliza's belly was huge. Regardless, since it was her aunt's sixth pending birth, Mary felt comfortable leaving the Shields' home shortly before Christmas for a visit to Cal's parents' home. Cal wanted Mary to see the progress that had been made on their future home, and his mother wanted to have a chance to get to know her future daughter-in-law. Other relatives were coming to visit Samuel and Eliza for Christmas, and Mary's absence would leave an extra bedroom available for guests.

On a nice day shortly before Christmas, Cal came for Mary, and they rode to his parents' home in excited anticipation of spending the holidays together. Cal's mother was every bit as warm, gracious, and welcoming as she had been when an exhausted eight year old Mary had arrived on her doorstep nine years prior. She greeted Mary with a warm hug and immediately remarked that she could see why Mary had captured her son's heart.

Cal's eight year old sister, Mary Elizabeth, seemed to be especially excited to meet Mary, and there was some teasing of Mary about the fact that the last time she was in the Nance home, she was the same age as Mary Elizabeth's current age. Cal remarked that on that occasion he had no idea he was meeting his future wife, and teased Mary about having to be carried up to bed that night. Then he impishly teased his mother by asking if he was going to be directed to carry Mary upstairs to bed again.

Sarah Nance was prompt in her admonishment. "You're twenty-eight years old, Calvin Nance. Behave yourself. Don't make me have to whip you."

Cal retorted that surely he could find a minister who would marry them on such short notice, and that remark brought on a mild rebuke from Mary.

"Then the whipping you'd get would be from my Aunt Eliza. She's already planning an elaborate wedding for us next spring."

With such bantering and jovial interaction, Mary felt thoroughly welcomed into the Nance family and enjoyed immensely the opportunity to get to know her future in-laws and Cal's siblings.

Mary had planned to return to Shields Station two days after Christmas, but a messenger came with a brief note from Doctor Sam suggesting that Mary prolong her visit with the Nance family until after the first of the year if it wouldn't be too much of an imposition to them. Mary wasn't at all unhappy about extending her visit and just assumed that the visitors to her aunt and uncle's home had decided to stay longer than originally planned. Elated to be near Cal for the extra time, Mary didn't suspect that the reason for the change in plans was not so simple.

When Mary did return home after the first of the year, she was horrified to learn of the events which had occurred in her absence. Grandmother Jane was there, and it was she who explained to Mary what had happened. Aunt Eliza had gone into labor just after midnight on Christmas Eve and had delivered a healthy baby boy a little after 3:00 a.m. The afterbirth followed shortly afterward, and the baby was soon put to breast. Despite vigorous nursing by the infant, the uterus remained large instead of decreasing in size as expected. Doctor Sam at first suspected retained clots, but an attempt to massage the uterus produced quite a surprise. Palpation of the abdomen revealed the clear outline of a second infant turned crosswise in the uterus. Doctor Sam attempted to force the baby to turn using external manipulation but was unsuccessful. Those manipulations seemed to increase the amount of blood loss, so the efforts to turn the baby were abandoned. Finally on the following day, Eliza was delivered of a stillborn infant.

Now, the first born infant was over a week old but was no longer nursing well and seemed to be struggling to breathe. Eliza was very ill, and Doctor

Sam suspected that she had an infection throughout her pelvic region.

On the day following Mary's return, the infant died. Grandma Jane and Mary bathed the baby and let Eliza hold him one last time before he was taken away for burial. Considering the severity of Eliza's illness, there was no wake, and only a handful of the closest kin attended the graveside service on a cold January day. Mary thought it the saddest possible beginning of a year that, for her, had held such promise of happiness.

Eliza slowly recovered her physical health over a period of several weeks, but her body seemed to recover much faster than her emotions. A pall hung over the home like the grey sky of a sunless winter day with Eliza confining herself entirely to her bedroom.

As winter began to release its grip on the countryside and the first signs of spring started to emerge, Grandma Jane announced that she must get home before spring rains turned the roads into a muddy quagmire. Before she left for home, she paused for a goodbye with Eliza. Mary was in the room, brushing her aunt's hair when Grandma Jane entered. Mary was somewhat taken aback by her grandmother's frankness.

"Eliza, you are both my niece and my daughter-in-law, and I love you dearly. Nevertheless, I am unwilling to hold back on what I'm about to say to you. Your body has healed, but your mind seems to be stuck on the loss of the babies. You've hardly been out of this room in the last three months. Of course you hurt, but you must not let this loss consume the rest of your life. It's not the first tragedy that has occurred in our family, and it won't be the last. Try to remember that you have five healthy children. They need a real mother, not a recluse who confines herself to her room. I'm leaving now, but you might begin this beautiful day that God has given us by coming downstairs, seeing the new greens of spring, and enjoying the sunshine as you see me off."

Having said all of that, Grandma Jane kissed Eliza on the forehead and left the room. Mary stood, silent, waiting to observe her aunt's response.

"I believe I have my marching orders, Mary. Please assist me down the stairs. I will see Mother Shields off."

Aunt Eliza never revealed to what extent the lecture from her mother-in-law had impacted her emotionally, but it did appear that day was a turning point in her recovery. From that day forward, she took her meals at the table with the rest of the family, questioned the children about their school progress, ventured outside to tend to her flowers, and checked on Emmie Lou's well-being. She also asked Cal for an update on the construction of his and Mary's home. With assurance that the house was nearing completion, Aunt Eliza announced in early April that she believed she and Mary needed to complete plans for a wedding.

With Cal's firm assurance that the house would be complete by early May, Mary opted for a late May wedding. She gave as her reason for the late May date her desire to celebrate her eighteenth birthday prior to her marriage and having roses in bloom for her bouquet and arrangements in the parlor. Secretly, her main concern was delaying her departure from Shields Station until after the birth of Emmie Lou's baby. She remained very concerned about an eleven year old giving birth.

Aunt Eliza's mood and spirit seemed to lift considerably as she focused on preparations for Mary's marriage to Cal. Mary said to herself that she would feel guilty about how much time her aunt was spending on the preparations except for the fact that her aunt seemed to be thriving under the stress of making a guest list, sending announcements, planning a menu, and making sure that Mary would be dressed beautifully.

In mid-April, a concerned Polly asked Doctor Sam if she could speak with him privately. Her concern was regarding who would deliver Emmie Lou's baby. Emmie Lou had told her mother she wanted a woman to help her with the birth. Polly said she didn't want to offend Doctor Sam, but she wanted to respect her little daughter's wishes if there was any way possible. Samuel assured Polly that he was not at all offended and suggested a midwife whose skills he respected.

"No, Polly, I'm not offended, and I think I can empathize with Emmie Lou in her desire to be attended by a woman. Rhoda Northern is an experienced midwife who has helped more babies come into the world than I have. She lives just a few miles from here, over in Jefferson County. I'll get a message to her, letting her know about this pending birth and the expected date. At the first sign of labor, we'll send for Rhoda. If she doesn't have other clients due about the time we expect Emmie Lou's baby, she might even be willing to arrive early and stay here for a few days. Even if she can't do that, please be assured that first labors usually are long enough to allow ample time for the midwife's arrival."

Rhoda Northern did agree to take Emmie Lou on as a client and even came by one day to meet her and discuss preparations for the birth. She said she did not make it a practice to move into a home prior to labor and reminded Polly again about first labors usually taking longer than subsequent births.

Meanwhile, Aunt Eliza continued preparation for the wedding, and Cal and Mary made a trip to Knoxville to purchase furniture for their home.

On Mary's birthday, May 3, Cal came for
dinner. After dinner, they sat by themselves on the
large back porch and talked about their anticipation of
their upcoming marriage.

"You know, Mary, all I can think about is you. It
seems like May 26 is taking forever to get here. I've
asked the minister to be here by noon although the
invitations say the ceremony will be at 1:00 p.m.
Hopefully he'll keep his remarks brief, we can have a
sumptuous meal that your aunt and Polly have planned,
and then we can head for home before it's too late in
the day."

"Sounds good to me, and I think preparation for
our wedding has been downright helpful for Aunt
Eliza. She's been so involved with all of this that I
can't imagine what she'll be like when one of her
children, especially one of the girls, marries."

While Mary and Cal sat talking, Polly came to
the door with an important announcement. Emmie Lou
was in labor. Sibby was with her but wondered if Mary
could come and offer her support also. Luke had been
sent to fetch Rhoda Northern and would accompany

her back for safety. It would undoubtedly be dark by the time Luke and the midwife would be on the last leg of the trip. Cal offered to stay, but Mary reminded him that it might be a very long wait.

Cal agreed then with Mary's assessment of the situation and said he would ride on home and be on the lookout for Luke and the midwife. "I can perhaps show them a shortcut across my property if they're willing to cut across a couple of fields." Cal gave Mary a quick peck on the cheek and left as Mary headed toward Polly's room.

Unbeknownst to Doctor Sam or anyone else in the household, Mary had read everything related to birth she could find in her uncle's medical books. She wasn't going to be the midwife, but at least she could be informed and aware of what to expect. When Mary got to Polly's room, she found Emmie Lou in bed. Immediately, Mary's knowledge from her reading kicked in.

"Emmie Lou doesn't need to be in bed this early in labor."

Sibby questioned her friend. "How do you know that?"

"I read it in one of my uncle's medical books. Emmie Lou's labor will likely be shorter if she walks around. Gravity helps the baby into position for the birth."

Mary spoke with such authority that neither Polly nor Sibby questioned her, and Emmie Lou seemed delighted to be permitted to be up and about for the time being.

As Emmie Lou paced the floor, she seemed relaxed during the first hours of labor. As she watched her sister pace, Sibby asked what would happen next. Mary had to admit that she didn't remember everything the book said.

Sibby wasn't ready to give up on the quest for more information. "Where is the book, Mary? Could you get it for us so we'll know what to expect next?"

Polly added her support for the idea although she did note that she had experienced labor twice and knew a little of what to expect.

Mary finally succumbed to the pressure to find the book. "The book is in Uncle Samuel's office, his medical dispensary in the front of the store. I remember what the book looks like, and I'll see if I can get it. If the door to his office is locked, I may not be able to get in unless he is still in the store. I'll see."

In a little while, Mary returned with the book and found the section dealing with the management of labor. As she had previously said, the book supported the practice of allowing the laboring woman to be up and about for as long as she felt comfortable doing that.

Hours passed, contractions were more frequent, and Emmie Lou was obviously more focused on her labor now. She alternated rubbing her belly and her lower back. Her little group of supporters had nothing to offer her except back rubs and efforts to distract her from the growing intensity of the labor.

Emmie Lou was the first to wonder aloud about the time and how soon they might expect the arrival of the midwife. Mary reassured Emmie Lou the best she could.

"I noticed the time on the tall clock in the old parlor when I went to get the book. It was almost 9:00 p.m. then. That's probably been close to an hour. Now, Emmie Lou, if the baby decides to arrive before the midwife gets here, I'm sure Doctor Sam will be happy to step in."

Tears appeared in Emmie Lou's eyes. "I want the midwife."

"I know that Emmie Lou, but you should find comfort in knowing that my uncle is here and can help you, if needed."

Polly added her agreement to that assessment. "Emmie Lou, the most important thing is that you and the baby come through okay. Doctor Sam would see to that."

The conversation was interrupted then by Emmie Lou asking for a pan to throw up in. Sibby whispered a question to Mary. "Is this normal?"

Polly overheard the question and responded, "I remember being sick in the last part of my labor. That's just part of it."

Sibby still wanted to know more. "Mary, what does the book say will happen next?"

Thus prodded, Mary began to read aloud from the book. "In the latter part of labor, the patient may be observed to experience nausea, vomiting, shaking of the limbs, perspiration, increasing amounts of bloody discharge, and complaints of extreme pressure in the pelvis. She may experience loss of control of the bowels. The physician or midwife should assure the patient that this intense portion of labor is the shortest. She should not be encouraged to push until her body urges her to do so as pushing prematurely can produce grave damage."

"Is that all it says, Mary?"

"The next part deals with the actual birth of the baby, Sibby."

Emmie Lou interrupted. "Where is the midwife? I want this to be over."

"I'm sorry, Emmie Lou. I guess we got involved with the book instead of you. I think what the book is saying is that your body knows exactly what to do if you'll just give it time."

"I think I'd like to lie down now if one of you will rub my back."

Mary took the lead. "Emmie Lou, let me help you to the bed. I'll be happy to rub your back."

Another hour passed. Emmie Lou had shown every one of the symptoms described in the medical book. Now, she seemed calmer, less stressed somehow, and then announced, "I have to push."

"Are you sure, Emmie Lou?"

A contraction hit. Emmie Lou squeezed Mary's hand hard. "I have to push; I can't help it."

"Emmie Lou, I think we ought to go get my uncle. Polly, would you go see if he's still up? Also, check the time on the way back if you would."

Polly returned in just a few minutes with less than reassuring news. Doctor Sam had been called out to see a very sick neighbor, and Eliza didn't know exactly when he would return.

Outwardly Mary remained calm and confident. Inside, all she could think of was, "Please, God, where is the midwife?" To Emmie Lou, she said, "Let me look and see if I see any sign of the baby yet."

Then turning to Sibby, Mary made yet another request. "Sibby, what does the book say happens next?"

"The book says when you first start seeing the head, you don't have to do anything. Then it says when you see the head staying against the peri…what's that word…press gently against the head so it doesn't emerge abruptly."

"That word is perineum, Sibby. It just means all the area down there, all the way back to the rectum."

Much to Mary's relief, it was at that precise moment that Rhoda Northern arrived and was escorted to the door by Luke. Mary quickly introduced Emmie Lou, Polly, and Sibby and then added, "and I'm Mary Graham, who was about to be the reluctant midwife."

As she set her things down, Miss Rhoda asked, "And what is going on now?"

Mary responded. "She's had the urge to push for about fifteen minutes now, but I don't see any sign of the head yet."

"Are the membranes still intact?"

"The bag of waters? I'm not sure. Emmie Lou may have peed in the bed a few minutes ago, or the waters may be leaking."

"I'm impressed. I have an idea that if I hadn't gotten here in time, you would have handled everything just fine."

A few minutes later, a fine baby boy arrived in the world. After he was dried and handed to his mother, Rhoda asked what the baby would be named.

"I'm naming him David, after David in the Bible. He was a shepherd boy, and he became a king. So, I think David is a good name."

Then Emmie Lou asked a question. "Is it midnight yet? I hope not. I wanted my baby born on Mary's birthday."

Chapter 7

Vows and More

The morning of May 26 dawned as beautiful as Mary had dreamed it would be. The sun was shining, there wasn't a cloud in the sky except for a few wisps floating by, and the air was just crisp enough to remind everyone that it was still spring, not summer. By the time Mary got downstairs, the big parlor was filled with bouquets of beautiful roses and peonies, perfuming the air with their intoxicating aroma. The lavish decorations may have been intended to be a surprise to Mary, but she couldn't resist a quick look.

After peeking into the room where she would say her vows later that day, Mary went to the dining room where breakfast was being laid out. William Graham had arrived the previous evening and was already seated at the table. He stood up as Mary entered to give her a hug. In the light of day, he looked older, more grey, to Mary than he had appeared to her on his arrival.

Mary sat down beside her father and awkwardly started a conversation. "This is my father," she thought, "but I feel as though I hardly know him."

"Daddy, I'm glad you came for my wedding. I didn't know if you would make it or not."

"I got here for Eliza's, didn't I? Did you think I would do any less for you? I do love you, you know?"

"Yes, Daddy, I know you love me, but it seems it takes a wedding to get you here."

"I know, honey; I'm sorry. Tell you what, I promise that when your first child is born, I'll come see that baby."

"Okay, Daddy, you'd better keep that promise. What was it you used to tell me when I was little? Promises made should be promises kept."

Conversation paused then for grace to be said before the meal. After grace, conversation moved onto other things including teasing Mary about not eating too much so she could fit into her wedding gown.

"It is pretty snug around the middle," agreed Mary, "but don't worry, I'll get in it. If I don't fit in it, Aunt Eliza will lace me up in a corset."

Everyone laughed, and conversation shifted to the weather, the time guests not yet present were expected to arrive, and the fact that Cal had instructed the minister to arrive an hour early.

"I think he wanted to make sure that nothing stopped the wedding from happening today. He proposed months ago. Guess he figures he's waited long enough."

Eliza spoke up. "Samuel, that's quite enough! Don't embarrass Mary."

"Mary, are you embarrassed?"

"No, Uncle Samuel, I'm not embarrassed, but I wouldn't admit it to this crowd if I were."

Grandmother Jane, who had arrived on the previous day, changed the subject completely then by saying it was too bad that Mary's sister couldn't come for the wedding.

Mary answered with a chuckle, "Well, how could she? She's been too busy having babies and nursing babies ever since she married five years ago. I told her then that she might wind up with eleven or twelve children getting married that young, and she reminded me that was a family tradition."

Samuel Shields couldn't resist teasing his mother. "Guess that includes you, Mother. You had eleven."

"Now don't get sassy with me, young man," came the quick retort.

Mary used that change in the conversation to excuse herself from the table. "I hate to leave this pleasant company so quickly, but I have packing to complete, and then Aunt Eliza wants to fix my hair in some fancy 'do-up' and get me gussied up for the ceremony."

The rest of the morning was pretty much a blur to Mary. Her aunt did pull her long dark hair back into an elaborate twist which Mary had to admit was quite attractive. "I'll tuck some tiny flowers in later, dear, after you're in your petticoats and dress. Now try not to do anything to mess up your hair as you dress," admonished Aunt Eliza as she stepped back to admire her handiwork.

"You're talking to me like I'm one of your little ones, Aunt Eliza. Maybe you need to go make sure Nanny Mabel is getting them ready."

"True! Although they're the ones who can't be gotten ready too early lest they're all messy and bedraggled looking before time for the wedding."

Finally, the packing was complete, and Mary was about to sit down for a minute when her aunt arrived again to say that it was time to dress for the ceremony. As Mary pulled on the last of the bouffant petticoats, she told her aunt, "I'm so glad I didn't let you talk me into another petticoat. I'll hardly be able to stand next to the guests as is."

"Well, just get into the dress, and let's see how you look."

Mary slipped the dress over her head, being careful not to mess up the arrangement of her hair.

Aunt Eliza fastened the tiny buttons which extended down the back of the cream colored silk dress.

"Oh, that is totally lovely, Mary, and your lace covered slippers are a perfect match to your collar and sleeves. Now, let me slip these tiny roses into the back of your hair, and you'll be ready to go downstairs. You can go down the back stairs and wait in the room beside the parlor until time for the ceremony."

"What time is it, Aunt Eliza?"

"It's 12:30 pm. John Howard is greeting guests at the front door and escorting them to the parlor. Janie, Lizzie, and Annie are dressed in their sweet little dresses and have their baskets of rose petals ready to scatter."

"I'm surprised there were any roses left for that. The parlor was full of bouquets when I peeked in this morning."

"Oh, we had plenty. In fact, the bushes are still loaded. For the loose petals, we used the roses that were about to shed. Now, enough talk. Get yourself downstairs. I think I hear the violinist playing."

The rest of the next hour was another blur to Mary: waiting in the side room briefly, both her father and her uncle coming to escort her into the parlor, Cal and the minister waiting at the front of the room, scripture read, vows quickly exchanged, and guests offering congratulations. Cal was constantly at Mary's side until he stepped away briefly and returned with a small plate of food.

Handing the plate to Mary, Cal whispered in her ear, "You need to eat. It's going to be a long day…and night." Mary looked up to see Cal grinning impishly. She smiled back, took the plate from is hand and replied, "Thank you, sir; I'll keep that in mind."

After an hour of mingling with the guests, Mary left the gathering to change clothes for the ride to her new home…her new life. She carefully hung her wedding dress in the wardrobe and set her slippers underneath. She changed into a casual blouse and skirt and riding boots, and removed the roses from her hair. Aunt Eliza had instructed her to leave the flowers behind for pressing into a keepsake.

As she passed through the small parlor, Mary noticed the time on the tall clock showed 3:30 p.m. She found Cal, also dressed for riding, talking with Mary's aunt and uncle and a few remaining guests. She waved to Cal and slipped away to the kitchen. There was one last goodbye to say.

As expected, Sibby was in the kitchen helping Polly.

"I couldn't leave without saying goodbye to you two. Where's Emmie Lou?"

"She and the baby are napping. We'll tell her bye for you."

"I'm going to miss you."

"You won't be that far away. We'll see you."

"Still my best friend, Sibby?"

"Always, Mary, always. And I might see you sooner than you know."

"What does that mean?"

Sibby just smiled like she had a secret. "Never mind. Just get out of here. You have a husband waiting."

With final goodbyes said to the remaining guests, Mary and Cal finally mounted the horses for the ride home.

"I would have liked to have brought the buggy for you, Mary, but some of the roads are just too rough. We're safer on the horses and can make better time too."

"I didn't see your parents and brothers as we left."

"They left earlier. Dad brought the wagon so he could transport wedding gifts and your trunk home. I admit though that I tried to talk my mother into going through your trunk and removing your nightgowns."

"You didn't!"

"Actually, I didn't, but I thought about it."

"Cal Nance, you are incorrigible!"

"You love me anyway?"

"I'm afraid I do, and you're stuck with me now."

"I like the sound of that."

"What will we do about supper? Is there even anything in the kitchen yet?"

"I thought we could just live on love for a few days."

"Cal, I don't know what I'm going to do with you."

"I have a few things in mind."

"Seriously, we'll need something to eat…Earlier, you said something about a long day and night."

"So I did, but don't worry about it. My mother is sending over two plates of food."

"Why didn't you just say so?"

"Because you're so much fun to tease, and I have to do something to pass the time until we get home. I'll show you the kitchen later."

As Cal and Mary neared his property, Cal suggested that they cut across through the field. With that shortcut taken, they were home more quickly than Mary had anticipated.

Supper did arrive as promised, delivered by one of Cal's brothers, but Mary scarcely remembered later what it was or how it tasted. Cal rinsed off the dishes at the cistern and left the plates on the porch as his mother had directed.

After the meal, Cal suggested a walk through the yard. "You might as well see the outside buildings, and I want you to see the river at sunset."

"Won't the sun be at our backs?"

"Mostly, yes, but there's something beautiful about the river with the light reflecting in it. If you want to see the sunset itself, you can look at it from the upper bedroom on the side opposite our bedroom. In our room, we'll get the sunrise."

"I like that, Cal. Did you plan it that way?"

"Yes, I wanted to be able to see the sunrise while holding my beautiful wife in my arms."

After a few more minutes strolling in the yard, Cal took Mary's hand and led her back to the house and up the stairs to their bedroom.

"I've waited a year, Mary."

"I know, Cal. Your wait is over."

In the morning, Cal woke first and left the bed briefly. When he returned, he crawled back into bed as the sun shone through the window, and wrapped Mary in his arms.

Later he told Mary, "You might as well leave on your nightgown."

Mary didn't say anything, just raised her eyebrows in question.

"Otherwise you might just have to undress again. It's a long time until tonight."

The sound of a bell ringing downstairs interrupted the conversation.

"Do you have a dressing gown or robe? Our breakfast is ready."

"I thought the meal delivery service was just for last night."

"Nope, my mother cooks for a crowd anyway. All my brothers are still at home. Plus there's my little sister and my parents – seven in all. So, what's two more? Let's go eat. I'm hungry."

Breakfast was on the table and still warm even though it would have been delivered from Cal's parents' home across the river. There was no sign of whoever had delivered the food.

"How much longer is our food to be delivered to us?"

"Don't worry about it. Just enjoy being pampered. You're used to Polly feeding you anyway. We'll tour the kitchen later this week."

"Will you let me out of my nightgown for that?"

"Yes, but be prepared for a surprise on that tour."

"What are you talking about?"

"My secret! Looks like I can't get you to quit asking questions unless I'm kissing you. So are you going to eat your breakfast or kiss me again?"

"I'll eat my breakfast, and then I'll kiss you."

"Are you glad you married me?"

"Yes, if I'd known last Christmas what marriage would be like, I might have encouraged you when you threatened to go find a minister."

Four days after the wedding, Cal said to Mary, "I guess you'd better put on some clothes. Today is the day to tour the kitchen."

"Is your mother tired of feeding us?"

"No, that isn't it. Just dress, and we'll tour the kitchen this afternoon."

When they got to the kitchen, Cal opened the door and said, "After you madam." Mary entered the room to find a fully equipped kitchen, complete with a new iron cooking stove from Mary's Uncle Milton's manufacturing plant in Morristown.

Cal took Mary by the elbow and steered her to the rear of the room, "There's one more thing you need to see." He knocked lightly on the door and then opened it before Mary could ask why he was knocking on the pantry door. There stood a smiling Sibby.

"What are you doing here, Sibby?"

As Mary reached to give Sibby a hug, she expressed her appreciation for seeing her friend. "Of course I don't mind you being here. We've been best friends for ten years, but I didn't expect to find you in the pantry of my kitchen."

"See, I told you on the day of your wedding that I'd see you soon."

Cal pointed beyond Sibby to the modest sized room behind her. "Mary, you didn't know that we could use the pantry as sleeping quarters also, but as you can see, it now contains a cot and a chest of drawers. Sibby is going to stay here and practice her cooking skills. You can help her as much you like just as you did at your Uncle Sam's place…Now, we need to get out of here and let Sibby finish unpacking. We'll see her again later."

As Cal and Mary turned to leave, Cal remarked to Sibby, "You let us know if you need anything."

Back at the house, Mary demanded to know what was going on. "Now please tell me, Cal, why Sibby is here. You didn't buy her, did you? You know how I feel about people owning slaves."

"Calm down, Mary. No, I didn't buy her. Technically, Sibby is still the property of your Uncle Sam. What I think you may not realize though is that your uncle has actually been a protector and provider for Polly and her family through the years. I think you told me that Polly indicated to you that she was once offered manumission before the 1834 law prohibited it completely for a time. She turned it down because she chose to stay with the Shields family. Isn't that true?"

"Yes, that is true, but I never thought about Uncle Samuel being a provider for Polly and her children."

"Tell me this. Does Polly work any harder than anyone else in the household except perhaps your aunt? Even she stays pretty busy attending to her children."

"That does paint things in a different light."

"There is one other thing you may not know. If Polly had accepted manumission, Tennessee law would have required her to leave the state within one year. Where would she have gone? What would she have done? Also, the Shields family was the only family she had known all her life… Now, I want to tell you the rest of what's 'going on' as you call it. Polly didn't exactly kick Sibby out, but she had told your uncle that her room was getting pretty crowded with her, Sibby, Emmie Lou, and now a baby, all sharing it. Also, I think you were so wrapped up in your concern for Emmie Lou and the preparations for our wedding that you hadn't observed another budding romance occurring almost under your nose."

"No, whose?"

"You know young Luke who helps in the inn and the store? He is really interested in Sibby. I believe he hopes that eventually she will be his wife. There's a problem there, however, because she's a Mulatto. Never mind that she's probably at least three-quarters white, according to law she is still a person of color and forbidden to legally marry a white person. Anyway, the color of Sibby's skin doesn't matter to Luke nor whether he is able to legally marry her or not. You may not have noticed that Luke himself is a little darker than some folks. He's from a community of people in Hancock County known as Melungeons. They have darker skin or olive skin, and some people think they're mixed race."

"Okay, I get that picture, but what does that have to do with Sibby being here?"

"It's perfectly alright with your uncle if Luke courts Sibby, but he doesn't think your aunt would approve. The deal is that I've hired Luke to work for me, he can see as much of Sibby as he wishes, and if they decide they want to make a life together, your uncle will give Sibby to Luke to carry off to his home community where she'll fit right in. He wants to save up enough money to buy some property first."

"It sounds almost like you've played Cupid."

"Well, not exactly, but do you feel any better now about Sibby being here?"

"Yes, I guess I do. Funny thing, when we were little things and I didn't know 'nothin' as Sibby said, I once told her that I hoped we could always live close together. She said for that to happen I'd have to buy her, and then she explained slave ownership to me."

"Well, your friend can live here close to you for now, but if Luke takes her away, you might never see her again."

"I'd miss her, but the main thing is I want her to be happy."

Chapter 8

Bonds

In the early days of marriage, Cal sometimes teased Mary with the question, "Do you think we've made a baby yet?" Mary usually responded with "You'll be the first to know," or "I don't know; you'll just have to keep trying." Mary did wonder if and when she might become a mother. She determined that in the meantime she would fill her time with useful activities such as tending to the large garden that had been planted near the house prior to their wedding.

Cal was often away from the house during the day with farming activities, leaving Mary and Sibby alone as they worked in the garden or preserved vegetables for winter consumption. Those hours of working together gave Mary a chance to ascertain how Sibby felt about Luke and to question Sibby as to why she had kept Mary in the dark about the budding romance.

Sibby pretty much confirmed everything Mary had been told by Cal but provided additional information that Cal hadn't known. Luke had already proposed to Sibby but said he did not want to take Sibby away to a different place to live until she was certain she could handle living so far from her mother and sister.

"He's afraid that I might not know myself well enough to be sure I can bear living where I might see my mother very rarely if at all. Also, he wants to be sure that I'm comfortable with having just a common law marriage since we can't wed legally. We know we can't marry here. Tennessee law won't allow it. However, Luke says if we go back to where he's from and he introduces me as his wife, there'll be no questions asked except where he found such a pretty wife."

"So, how do you feel about that, Sibby?"

"I'm thinking I'm willing to do that, but I haven't given him an answer yet."

"What does your mother think?"

"I think she believes it's a good idea. She said at least my children would have a father, a real father as she called it. So, like I said, I'm thinking about it, but I'm not going anywhere yet. You have to put up with me a while longer."

"I wouldn't call it that, Sibby. Cal is gone most of the day, tending to the farm, and having you here gives me somebody to talk to."

"Maybe you'll soon have a baby to talk to."

"I hope so, but I don't think that will be like talking to my best friend."

Talking to her friend, tending a garden, and enjoying her marriage to Cal, Mary passed the summer in her new role as wife. Fall brought some new challenges that Mary hadn't encountered previously – drying apples, helping make cider, and helping prepare meat for preservation. As winter settled in, Mary turned to needlework to occupy a good portion of her time.

It was a couple of weeks before Christmas that Mary began to suspect that she might be expecting a baby. She waited until Christmas day to share her suspicion with Cal.

When Cal heard the news, he responded with unmitigated enthusiasm. "That's the best Christmas present ever! How long have you known?"

"I just started to suspect a couple of weeks ago. We'll know soon."

The second person Mary told was Sibby, whose response was almost as enthusiastic as Cal's had been. "Oh, Mary, that is wonderful. Now, aren't you glad that your Aunt Eliza made you work on your sewing skills? You'll be making baby clothes all winter."

"Aunt Eliza taught me fancy stitches and how to make a beautiful sampler to hang on the wall. She didn't teach me how to make a garment. I don't think she had much of an idea how to do that herself. At least, she hired seamstresses to come in and sew for the family. Maybe my mother-in-law can help me learn some more practical sewing skills."

By early summer, baby clothes and blankets were prepared and ready for the big day which was expected to occur in August. Cal reminded Mary that she needed to select someone to assist her in labor. "Are you going to have your uncle deliver the baby? He has welcomed a lot of babies into the world."

"No, I do not want my uncle to help me. I love my uncle, and he was a second father to me for ten years, but precisely because of that fact, I want someone else. I want Rhoda Northern."

"Remember, she almost didn't make it in time for Emmie Lou. You almost became, as you said, the reluctant midwife."

"I know, Cal, but our home is several miles closer to where she lives than where she had to come to assist Emmie Lou. Although she barely arrived in time, I was impressed with her. Please send a message to her, or speak to her yourself, and let her know that our baby is expected in late August."

Baby Sarah Jane arrived on August 28 with Rhoda Northern serving as midwife and Sibby and Cal's mother there to offer encouragement and support. The baby was named for Cal's mother and Mary's grandmother, Jane Shields. A few hours after the baby's birth, Mary sat holding and admiring the newborn and thinking how blessed she was. She said to Cal, "Have you ever seen anything so precious?"

"Only her mother," was Cal's quick reply.

News of the baby's birth was sent to Mary's father, and he did come for a visit as he had promised. He brought with him a small blue highchair he had built for the baby. "Oh, Dad, I will treasure this little chair forever. My children and grandchildren will sit in this chair. It is precious. Thank you for making it, and especially, thank you for coming to see us. I hope you'll be able to stay a few days."

"Not that long, I'm afraid. I need to get back to tend to the store. Please forgive me. I promised you I would come see you when your first child was born, so I thought I'd better keep that promise. I do have to leave tomorrow."

Shortly after Sarah Jane's birth, Sibby told Mary that she was certain she wanted to spend the rest of her life with Luke even though they could not legally wed.

"I'm going to miss you, Sibby."

"I'll miss you, too, Mary, but we can write. Now aren't you glad you taught me how to read and write over ten years ago?"

Sibby's departure left Cal and Mary without anyone to do the cooking for the family. Mary opined that she was a good cook and could take over that responsibility, but Cal had severe reservations.

"Mary, you're nursing a newborn infant and getting up during the night to feed her. I can't have you getting up and going out to the kitchen early in the morning to make breakfast. If I'm out tending to farm chores, you'd have to take Sarah with you. I thought I was being smart when I built the kitchen and pantry as a freestanding building. Now, that choice doesn't seem as wise. Anyway, I'm going to look for someone else to do the cooking and maybe help some with household chores."

"Are you talking about a slave, Cal? You know my feelings about that."

"Yes, I know, but you were alright with Sibby being here, and she was still owned by your uncle. "

"Well, he freed her though, didn't he?"

"Not really. He sold her to Luke so he would have some claim to her in case he was ever questioned about her being with him."

"Regardless, I still don't want you to purchase a slave."

"Could I borrow one from my parents?"

"Please see if you can come up with some other option, Cal."

Soon after, Cal found a young woman from Jefferson County who had lost both parents to illness and needed a way to provide for herself. Cal offered the young woman a job cooking for the family and assisting with the garden, and she gladly accepted. The girl, named Rena, moved into the pantry to live. She wasn't Sibby, but her cooking skills were good, and she was a willing worker.

As Mary watched little Sarah grow and develop and do all the cute things that babies do, she was amazed at the intensity of her feelings for her little daughter. She shared her feelings with Cal. "Back when I was helping with Aunt Eliza's babies, I loved them so much that I couldn't imagine loving a child of my own more, but I do. There's just no comparison. I take delight in everything this little one does, and when she holds out her little arms to me, I just melt. I look at that precious little face and think she's a gift straight from Heaven."

"Yes, I know, Mary. Next to her mother, she's the most precious person I know."

By the time that little Sarah was eighteen months old, Mary began to suspect that she was expecting another baby. Again, she waited until Christmas to give Cal the news. Once again, he was excited by the news and remarked there must be something about the first cool weather of autumn that helped with baby making.

Cal and Mary welcomed their first son into the family on July 4, 1846. They named him Samuel Shields for Mary's uncle and decided they would call him Shields. Mary told Cal that it seemed strange to be holding a small newborn after being accustomed to dealing with Sarah who was now almost three, but she found him to be equally as precious as her first born. At first, it seemed to be a big challenge to take care of both the newborn and a toddler, but Sarah was a helpful child and seemed to love the baby. Mary was grateful for that, and grateful that they had Rena to do the cooking and help with the garden.

In a little less than two years, Mary found herself pregnant again, but this baby hadn't waited for an autumn conception. This baby was obviously conceived in the spring as Mary began to suspect pregnancy in the early summer of 1848. Like her other two pregnancies, everything went well, and a second son was born December 14, 1848, and named John William for Cal's father and Mary's father. Mary thought it nice that the two boys would be close enough in age to be good friends and playmates growing up.

Baby John was very small when Mary received news that her grandmother Jane had died. While the news made Mary sad, she took solace in the fact that her grandmother had lived to eighty-five years of age and had lived the kind of life that had impacted so many people in a positive way. She thought of how her grandmother had been so kind when her mother had died and how she had seemed to say just the right thing to Aunt Eliza after the death of the twins. Mary was also glad that her grandmother had lived long enough to have known about several babies, including her own Sarah Jane, having been named for her.

Shortly after John's birth and the death of Mary's grandmother, Cal came to Mary with a proposal that required real soul searching. Polly wanted Emmie Lou and little David in a safer place than Shields Station. She thought Emmie Lou, now eighteen, was too attractive to some of the gentlemen staying at the inn, and she was dreadfully afraid that someone might see David playing in the yard and snatch him up and carry him away to be sold, just like what had happened to Emmie Lou's dad. Polly had shared her worries with Doctor Sam, and he had made Cal an offer. He wanted to sell Emmie Lou and David to Cal because he thought they would be loved and kept safe with Cal and Mary.

"Why can't Uncle Sam just free them?"

"To be perfectly honest, Mary, your uncle needs a little extra money to help John Howard with a business venture in Knoxville, plus the manumission laws are getting even trickier than they have been for the last twenty-five years. Remember, your uncle didn't free Sibby. He sold her to Luke. I know it seems weird, but some free black men are resorting to owning their own wives and children to keep them safe. So, please think about this, and we'll talk some more about it later."

The next day, without any further discussion, Mary announced her decision to Cal.

"I still don't believe in slavery, Cal, but it does seem like, under the circumstances, that bringing Emmie Lou and David here is the best thing to do. If that requires giving my uncle some money and signing a paper, then do it...Oh, and by the way, have you thought about where you're going to put them? Are you going to crowd both of them into that little room that is actually a pantry or what?"

"Emmie Lou has lived her entire life in your aunt and uncle's house. I don't know how comfortable she would be in a separate cabin, although we could certainly build one for her."

"Cal, let's talk to Emmie Lou and see what she prefers."

A couple of days later, Cal rode over to Shields Station to finalize arrangements with Doctor Sam and to talk with Emmie Lou. Mary was surprised to learn on Cal's return that Emmie Lou said she preferred to live in the small room next to the kitchen with a separate cabin a possibility in the future.

Emmie Lou moved in within the week and assumed responsibility of cooking for the family. On arrival, she told Mary, "I've never felt completely safe at Shields Station since I was attacked there. Too, I feel good about moving here because of the way you helped the night David was born. You kept everybody calm. Also, you've been a good friend to Sibby through the years. So, I think this move is for the best."

Finally, Mary felt at peace about the decision to bring Emmie Lou and David to their home, but she refused to call them slaves. To her, they were just family members whose skin happened to be darker than hers. In the early fall, when a census worker came for a visit, getting an advance start on the 1850 census, Mary reluctantly reported ownership of a nineteen year old female slave and an eight year old male, the ages they would be in 1850. She hated the very idea of them being labeled as slaves, not even called by name on the census worker's form, but just listed by gender and age.

The week after the census worker's visit, Mary's father came for a visit, his first since little John's birth. Upon arrival, he was greeted by David.

"And who is this fine young man?" William inquired of Mary.

After Mary explained to her father the circumstances of Emmie Lou's and David's arrival and her personal distress at being a slave owner, he laughed and said, "Wait until you hear my story. I'm also a slave owner now. Thirteen slaves actually."

"But you've always been opposed to slavery, Daddy. What is going on?"

"My personal values haven't changed, Mary, but strange circumstances pushed me into an ownership I neither sought nor desired."

"So how under the sun did you become the owner of thirteen of your fellow human beings?"

"It's sort of a long story, but I'll try to make it brief. An older man had run up a large tab at the store. He was in very poor health, as was his wife. They planned to sell their little bit of property and move to their son's home near New Market. The son is of the Quaker persuasion and said his father could not bring his slaves under any circumstances. So the elderly gentleman begged me to take the Negroes in lieu of payment of his bill. He didn't want to sell them to someone else for fear they would be abused. I refused to give him an answer at first until I learned more about the situation. It turns out his thirteen slaves consist of a man, his wife, and eleven children. The oldest child can hardly be called a child, but he is the son of the forty-five year old man. The father lost his first wife some years ago and married a mulatto girl fifteen years his junior, and they have produced ten children thus far, ranging in age from fifteen to a one year old infant. The ten children include a set of twins."

"Where are they living, Dad, and what are they doing?"

"The gentleman is helping me in the store, and the two oldest boys make runs for supplies and deliveries. All are good workers. I pay them a salary just as though they're free. The wife takes care of the garden and prepares a meal for me when she is cooking for the family."

"You still didn't say where they are living, Dad."

"Oh, sorry; they're living in the house. No need for it to sit there empty any longer. It's been seventeen years since I lived in it. Now it's filled with a bunch of lively, happy children. I believe they think I'm their grandfather; they call me Pa Graham."

"Little children don't see skin color, Dad. For them, you are like a grandfather."

"Speaking of being a grandfather, where is the newest member of your family? I would like very much to meet him now."

Chapter 9

The Rescue

The day after Mary's father left to return home, Cal announced to Mary that he needed to make a trip to Dandridge with his father. "Dad wants me to go with him to Dandridge tomorrow to witness a business transaction – a land transfer to one of my brothers. If we leave early in the morning, we should be back before dark. Do you need anything picked up?"

"I do need some flannel for nightgowns and winter shirts. If you pick that up, it would save a trip over to Shields Station."

"Sure. How much do you want?"

"I know it sounds like a lot, but I need at least forty yards."

"Your wish is my command. What colors do you want?"

"That doesn't particularly matter except remember that some of the material will be used for two or three new shirts for you."

"I need to pick up some supplies for the farm, too, so I'll take the wagon. Taking the wagon will slow us down some, but I still think we can make it back by dark."

"The days are getting shorter, Cal."

"Last I checked every day still had twenty-four hours, Mary."

"You know what I mean; the daylight hours are getting shorter."

"I know, but you're still fun to tease."

"Is that why you married me – to have someone to tease?"

"No, three children to our credit is proof I had something else in mind. Nevertheless, I guess I'd better quit teasing you now and make preparations for the trip tomorrow. I'll let Emmie Lou know that I'll need breakfast early."

The following morning, Cal did leave early, just as baby John awakened, wanting to be fed. Cal kissed both Mary and the baby as he left, posing a final question, "You did say you wanted forty yards of flannel?"

"Yes, I need at least forty yards. If it feels like good sturdy fabric, get fifty yards. It doesn't hurt to have extra on hand."

"Okay. See you about sunset, ma'am."

With Cal gone and the two older children still asleep, Mary sat in the rocker, nursing the baby and enjoying the quiet peace of the morning. At not quite nine months, John was eating a lot of table food, but he still very much enjoyed nursing, especially the first thing every morning and the last thing at night. The early morning feeding time was special to Mary also. She enjoyed the sensation of the baby nursing, and she often sang little songs to the baby as he nursed. This morning, instead of singing, she listened to the twitter of birds in the trees outside. Speaking aloud, ostensibly to the baby but more to herself, she asked, "Wonder what the birds are saying to each other? Do you think they are lamenting the fact that summer is at end?"

The baby, content to be cuddled and fed, made no response to his mother's musings. When he wasn't nursing, he was quite responsive to adults talking to him and often babbled back in his own unique language. Mary loved watching the development of each of her children, each one a little different. John was crawling really well, pulling up to the sides of his crib, and saying "Ma-ma" and "Da-da" with great enthusiasm. The meaning of his other babbling was quite unintelligible. If it had meaning, only he knew.

When she had finished feeding the baby, Mary put him back in the crib while she dressed. Then she took all the children downstairs to the dining room for the breakfast Emmie Lou had prepared. Mary invited Emmie Lou and David to join them for the meal. David was only fifteen months older than Sarah, and the two had become good playmates since Emmie Lou's arrival. During breakfast, Mary broached the subject of schooling to Emmie Lou, asking what if anything had been done about teaching David to read.

"I haven't done anything. You taught both Sibby and me to read, but I didn't know whether to teach David or not. Seems like a lot of folks are afraid of teaching slaves to read, thinking it gives them too much power or something."

"Well, you know I don't feel that way, Emmie Lou, and I don't even like the fact that you're called a slave. You and Sibby both are like sisters to me, and to this day, Sibby is my best friend in the world. I'm glad she lives in a place now where she's just Luke's wife, not a slave, but I sure do miss her…Before I get caught up though in talking about how much I miss Sibby, let's get back to the schooling issue. Sarah is six years old and knows her ABCs. I had Cal buy a couple of basic readers and a children's story book the last time he was over to Shields Station. I'm going to start teaching Sarah to read and would love to teach David also."

"Oh, Mary, that is wonderful. I'm glad you want to do that."

"Good! How about I get started on that this afternoon while Shields and John are napping? If they wake up before I'm finished with the lesson, maybe you can watch them for a few minutes. You should have time for that before you start supper, shouldn't you?"

"Yes ma'am. I'll be proud to help that way. There isn't that much left to do in the garden, so I sure should have time to help watch the little ones for a while."

After the lesson was completed in the afternoon, Sarah asked if she and David could play outside until suppertime.

"Yes, you may play outside, but stay away from the cliff, Sarah. It's dangerous."

"Daddy said he and his brothers used to cross the ferry and play on the cliff by holding onto saplings."

"I wish your daddy hadn't told you that, but if he and his brothers did that, they were probably older than you are. So stay off the cliff! Do you understand me?"

"Yes ma'am. We'll just play in the lane and the front yard."

"Promise?"

"I promise."

"Okay. Then run and play, and if you happen to see your daddy getting on the ferry, come and let me know. That way I can let Emmie Lou know about getting supper on the table."

It was nearly 6:00 p.m. when Sarah and David came running with the news that they had spotted the wagon about to cross the river on the ferry. "Daddy is coming across the river now with the wagon. Grandpa is coming across, too, but he's just riding his horse across. I guess the water is pretty low. Oh, and it looks like there's an extra person in the wagon."

"An extra person? I don't know who that would be. I wonder if your daddy is bringing someone home for supper...Regardless, you two get washed up. I hear baby John waking up, and I need to get him. He'll be wanting to eat. Shields is surely awake from his nap also."

The children went off to wash up for supper, and Mary gave no more thought to who the occupant of the wagon might be. She went upstairs, changed John's diaper and carried him downstairs as three year old Shields followed, chatting about a story his mother had read him before his nap.

As Mary sat down to nurse John in the downstairs bedroom, she heard Cal speaking to Sarah and David, and then he came to the bedroom. He spoke, kissed Mary on the forehead, and pulled up another chair beside the rocker where Mary was seated.

"You look worried, Cal. Is something wrong?"

"Well, that depends on your reaction to what I'm about to tell you, but please hear me out. I think you'll understand…After Dad and I finished with the business and I had bought the flannel and the farm supplies, we went to get something to eat. When we were about to pay for our food before leaving, a bit of a row erupted. A very drunk man came in wanting something to eat. The proprietor told him in no uncertain terms that he wasn't going to serve him, considering the condition he was in. Then the man asked if he could at least have some water for the girl he had tied up out front and started bragging about how he'd found someone who could serve as a wife since his wife had run off and gone back to her pa. We stuck around for a minute to make sure the proprietor didn't need any help, and as he escorted the man outside, we exited the building also."

"Well, I'm glad you managed to have a nice meal before all that happened."

"Yes, but that isn't the half of it, Mary. Sure enough, just like the man had bragged, there was a young Negro woman tied to a hitching post like she was an animal of some kind. Around here, we don't see that kind of behavior. Maybe some places, but not here! Mary, all I could think of was how upset you would be if you saw a person being treated like that. So, without thinking twice, I asked the drunk man how much he had paid for the girl. He was so drunk that he didn't seem to remember at first how much he had paid. Then, he pulled a bill of sale out of his pocket, saying he hadn't even registered the sale yet. I offered him fifty dollars more, he accepted the offer, and I drug him over to the courthouse to register the sale. Oh, I guess I left out one thing; I first untied the girl and got her some food from the restaurant. Dad stayed with her while I took the drunk to the courthouse."

"So that was who was in the wagon?"

"Yes, I've tried to assure her that she's safe here, but as you can imagine, she's pretty distraught. Emmie Lou is helping her get cleaned up and finding some clean clothes for her. Then I'll bring her to meet you. Oh, I forgot to say; she says her name is Lucy."

In a few minutes, Cal returned with Lucy, an attractive young woman who appeared to be in her early twenties, at most.

"Lucy, this is my wife. She's anxious to meet you. I'm going to let you two get acquainted while I wash up and get ready for supper. It smells like Emmie Lou has something good fixed."

Mary gestured to the empty chair Cal had vacated and spoke first to Lucy. "Have a seat. Lucy. I'm Mary. I hope you don't mind if I finish nursing the baby while I get to know you. From what my husband told me, you've had quite a bad experience. I know my husband has tried to reassure you, but I want to also tell you that you're safe now. We do not mistreat people here."

At first, Lucy made no response. She looked at Mary's face for several seconds as though making a judgment about her character, her trustworthiness. Then she spoke.

"When you finish nursing, could I hold the baby for a minute?"

"Certainly. I think baby John is about finished. He noticed a different voice in the room and is trying to see who you are."

Mary removed John from her breast and handed him to Lucy, saying as she handed him over, "He doesn't see a lot of new people, so don't be offended if he doesn't want anything to do with you at first."

Mary was pleasantly surprised to see that the baby did not appear to be afraid of the newcomer, just curious perhaps. He allowed her to cuddle him for a few moments before squirming to be let down. Once down on the floor, he returned to his mother's knee and pulled himself to a standing position.

Mary looked up at Lucy's face and saw tears streaming down her cheeks. Simultaneously, she observed two damp circles on the front of the clean dress provided to her only minutes before.

"Lucy, I hate to pry, but I don't know any way to ask this without being blunt. Did you recently lose a baby?"

Lucy shook her head no, but the tears continued to flow as Mary refused to stop her line of questioning.

"I'm a mother. This is the third baby I've nursed. I'm not blind to your leaking breasts. Now, please tell me what is going on."

Mary handed her handkerchief to Lucy. "Please!"

Lucy wiped her eyes and her nose, and finally told her story. "I barely know you -- just got here a few minutes ago, but you seem different from any white woman I've ever known. So for some reason, I trust you…I have twin babies – George and Henry. They weren't of my choosing, if you know what I mean, but they're my babies, and I love them. Anyways, they weren't even six weeks old when my owner's no account son came sneaking into my cabin whilst I were cooking supper. He started taking his pants off, and I picked up the nearest thing I could get my hands on and heaved it at him. That big stick of firewood struck him right above the eye. Right good lick, too! He went screaming out, one hand holding his bleeding head and one hand trying to hold up his pants. 'Course I got punished, but I was determined no man was ever going to take advantage of me again! Not if I could help it."

"So, where are your babies, Lucy?"

"Well, after that boy went crying to his pappy, I was beat on my back with a riding crop, and the old man said I was gonna be sold. They tied me up overnight, wouldn't even let me nurse my babies. My friend with a baby said she'd try to take care of them, but I don't see how she'll have enough milk for three babies. Anyway, they hauled me into town the next day, locked me up overnight in some building without one bite of food, and the next day I was sold to that drunk I was with when your husband and his daddy found me."

"Was that in Dandridge where you were sold?"

"No, I think it was Morristown."

"Lucy, supper is on the table. Let's go into the dining room and sit down for some supper. I want Cal to hear the rest of your story."

"You mean you is inviting me to sit down at your table and eat a meal with you?"

"Yes, Lucy, that is precisely what I'm saying. Now come on; let's go have some supper."

After the blessing was said, Mary gave Cal the condensed version of Lucy's story, using terms Cal could understand without saying things she didn't want Sarah to hear. After learning about the twins, Cal assured Lucy that he would do everything he could to get them back for her. He asked for her former owner's name before remembering that he had the man's name on the bill of sale. He also got the best directions Lucy could provide and then told Mary that he had an errand to run after supper. When he returned from the errand, Cal announced that he was going to leave early the next morning to go look for the babies. His brother Noah would accompany him.

"Noah and I will leave early in the morning. We'll take the buggy because I don't want to try to bring two babies home on horseback. Morristown isn't much further than Dandridge, so if we find this place without any trouble, we may be able to make this a one day trip. If we have any delay in finding the place, we might have to spend the night at either your sister's place or your Uncle Milton's place."

"Do be careful, Cal."

"I will be, Mary. I'll go armed, but I don't think the man is likely to give us any trouble. I'll have money to pay him, and money speaks louder than anything else to his kind. If necessary, I'll throw some names around so he'll know that I have connections with people in the area who would come looking for me if I went missing."

"I hope you're right about no trouble being likely. See if Emmie Lou will pack some food for you."

"Good idea. I'll go speak to her now."

After Cal left to go speak with Emmie Lou, Lucy said to Mary, "Nobody has ever treated me like this before. I can't believe Mr. Cal is gonna go try to buy my babies."

"He's a good man, Lucy. That's why I married him. Now I need to get the children to bed and get ready for an early bedtime myself. Would you like to spend the night in the bedroom where we sat and talked before supper?"

"I appreciate that ma'am, but Emmie Lou offered earlier for me to share her room tonight. Said she'd make David a pallet on the floor so I could have his bed. She said she'd tend to my sore back again, too. So if you don't mind, that's what I'd like to do."

"No, I don't mind that at all, Lucy. I didn't know she had made that offer. Do I need to look at your back? If it looks too bad, I could send someone over to ask my Uncle Samuel, a doctor, to come see you."

"I don't think that's needed. Most of it is just welts and bruises, not open places, and Emmie Lou said it looked to her like it was healing. She took a good look at it when she helped me get cleaned up when I first got here. She was talking to me so nice the whole time, telling me how I'd like it here. She even told me how you almost delivered David when he was in a hurry to arrive before the midwife."

"I didn't realize Emmie Lou had that much time with you, but I'm glad you seem to like her. She's been part of my life since she was just a baby crawling on the floor of her mother's kitchen…Oh, by the way, Lucy, tomorrow we'll see about finding some more clothes for you."

"If you've got any cloth, I'm right good with a needle and thread."

"I'm glad to hear that, Lucy. Cal just bought fifty yards of flannel for me today for winter shirts and nightgowns. Maybe you can help me with those. Now if you'll excuse me, I'll tell you good-night and let you go find Emmie Lou."

In Cal's absence the following day, Mary tried to occupy herself by finding some fabric suitable for a couple of simple dresses for Lucy. She was happy to discover that Lucy was indeed a talented seamstress. Together, the two women occupied their time when Mary wasn't tending to the two youngest children or having her afternoon lesson with Sarah and David. When Mary started the lesson with the children, she asked Lucy if she had ever been taught to read and write. Upon hearing a negative answer, she invited Lucy to join the little class in the library. "Well, you're not too old to learn. I'll do a bit of review today to help you get started catching up. Just pull up a chair."

Aloud, Lucy declared, "Lordy, I think I done died and went to Heaven!"

Late in the day, both Mary and Lucy began to wonder if Cal would make it home that day and if he would have the twins with him. Finally, Mary invited Lucy to accompany her to her upstairs bedroom to use the spyglass to watch the road across the river for any sign of the men returning. Mary reminded Lucy that Cal had said his mission might take two days. That message did nothing to deter Lucy's determined watch. Even when Emmie Lou came upstairs to announce that supper was ready, Lucy didn't want to stop using the spyglass. Mary was about to leave anyway to have her supper, when Lucy exclaimed, "I see them; I see them," and flung the spyglass onto the bed.

As Mary and Emmie Lou watched in amazement, Lucy darted out the side door and headed straight down the cliff, the most direct route to the ferry landing.

If Lucy heard Mary's screams, she ignored them. Mary could only shake her head and say to Emmie Lou, "I hope she doesn't kill herself on that cliff."

Lucy was out of view for a while, and the ferry landing was also out of view. When Mary and Emmie Lou saw Lucy again, she was coming up the cliff, a baby under each arm like a sack of flour. Mary could only shake her head in disbelief. "I don't know how she did that. Children have been known to climb that cliff holding onto saplings. That girl just climbed it with a baby under each arm."

Emmie Lou chimed in. "Look, Mary; she's not even out of breath."

"Emmie Lou, can you hold supper for a few minutes? I'll help Lucy tend to the babies while Cal brings the buggy up the road, the way most people arrive at this house…Lucy, hand me one of the babies, and let's go in the house. These babies must be starving even if they were fed by your friend in the middle of the day. They also need clean diapers. I'll grab a couple and some cleaning cloths." As soon as the crying babies were cleaned and diapered, Lucy sat down to feed them but almost immediately announced that she was afraid she didn't have enough milk for both of them.

"I've been away from my babies for four days. My breasts don't feel like I have enough milk for both of them. I usually feed Henry first because he's harder to feed, but George is so hungry he's screaming his head off."

"Lucy, your milk supply will come back. In the meantime, let me feed George."

"You would feed my baby?"

"Yes, I'm going to feed your baby. Now hand over George. I doubt that he'll care that a white woman is nursing him."

Soon both babies were settled in, happily getting their tummies filled. When both were satisfied to the point of falling asleep, Mary helped Lucy tuck both babies into the large cradle Mary kept downstairs for use when her babies were small.

"Now, let's go have some supper ourselves, Lucy. Nursing mothers need food, too. While we eat, maybe Cal will tell us about his day and finding your babies."

"Miss Mary, I didn't know there were people like you. First Mr. Cal rescued me from that awful man who had plans to 'use me like a wife' as he said. Then today, he found my babies and brought them to me, and to top it all, you fed George for me. No, I didn't know there were people like you. I don't know how to thank you."

"You just did. Now, please, let's go eat. I'm starving. After we eat, we can talk about sleeping arrangements for tonight. I'm suggesting that you let

George sleep in the cradle in my bedroom in case he needs to be fed during the night. You and little Henry can either sleep downstairs in the room where we fed the babies, or you can sleep upstairs in the guest bedroom with Henry in a make-shift bed in a dresser drawer. Tomorrow, we can borrow another cradle from Cal's parents' home or one of his brothers."

All Cal would say at supper about his day was that it had gone about as he expected and that he had experienced no trouble in finding Lucy's previous owner. Then he grinned and said, "Oh, Lucy, I forgot to tell you; I saw a young fellow slinking around with a big ol' gash above his eye. I gave him a good stare down for you."

After everyone was settled in for the night, Cal told Mary the rest of the story. The former owner was so easy to find because everyone seemed to know who he was and thought he was a jerk.

"How much did you have to pay the jerk to get Lucy's babies?"

"Oh, about the going rate for a strong, healthy young man in his prime -- $1,000 each."

Chapter 10

Life Abundant

Lucy's addition to the household proved to be of immense value to Mary. She was an excellent seamstress and more than willing to help with household chores and child care. Meanwhile, she seemed to be eternally grateful to be in a place where she was treated with respect. Several times she mentioned to Emmie Lou her astonishment that Mary had insisted on feeding baby George for a few days and that she was being taught to read and write. Emmie Lou passed these comments on to Mary.

Even though Mary's basic view on slavery had not changed, she reluctantly accepted the fact that, given the circumstances of the day, both Lucy and Emmie Lou were far better off than in their previous situations, especially Lucy. Furthermore, she recognized that Cal was right about manumission. Giving these young women their freedom would require them to leave the state within a year. Where could they go? What could they do to support themselves and their children? Here, they had food, shelter, clothing, and medical attention if needed. Mary was well aware of the groups springing up in opposition to slavery and was strongly supportive of the goal of the abolitionists. She thought, however, that some of the ideas being proposed were ridiculous, especially the one advocating for freeing the slaves and putting them on boats back to Africa.

Lucy and her babies spent the winter in the guest bedroom. In the spring, a cabin was built that was large enough to accommodate Emmie Lou and David and Lucy and her twins. When plans for this arrangement were first discussed, Lucy was assured that she could bring the twins with her each day to the main house. Emmie Lou, who had initially preferred living in the cramped quarters of the kitchen pantry, was also pleased with the arrangement. Furniture was found for the new dwelling, Lucy made curtains, and both young women seemed to take great pride in making their home attractive.

As spring turned into summer and garden produce demanded attention, it was often advantageous for Lucy to help with the garden while Mary watched the twins. It was while watching the twins that Mary began to suspect that something wasn't quite right about baby Henry. He was about the same size as his twin, but at nine months, he could barely sit up by himself. He also didn't seem to be interested in the typical interactive games such as pat-a-cake and hide the face. Mary was hesitant to say anything to Lucy, but she did wonder if Lucy was aware of the difference in development between the two babies.

Finally, Mary did decide to ask Lucy if Henry ever tried to make babbling noises or say "Ma-ma." Lucy's response was a surprise to Mary.

"No ma'am, but he's been different ever since he was born. He was the first one to try to come out, and he came feet first. The woman trying to help me had never seen anything like it. At first, she said something like 'Oh lordy, this baby has toes growing out of his head.' Then she realized the toes were attached to feet, and the feet were attached to legs. Soon, the whole body was out except the head. The head was stuck, and the woman didn't know what to do. I don't know how long it took; it seemed like forever. Another woman came in and twisted on the baby or something, and I pushed real hard, and he finally came out. He didn't cry at first and was a funny color – all greyish blue. I was still trying to have the second baby, but I think they just wrapped him in warm towels and blew in his mouth. So he's always been different. Remember when I first got here I told you that I usually fed Henry first. That was because he didn't even nurse well."

All Mary could say was, "I'm so sorry, Lucy. We'll do all we can for Henry and hope that, with time, he'll improve. I can ask my uncle, Doctor Sam, to take a look at him sometime."

Mary did have her uncle examine little Henry, but he could not offer much hope. "From what Lucy says, it's pretty clear this baby didn't breathe soon enough when he was born. He's probably always going to be not quite right. Hopefully, he will improve some, but there's nothing that any doctor can do,"

It was obvious to Mary that Lucy had accepted that Henry was different and would always be less than normal. Still, being the optimist that she was, Mary emphasized the positive to Lucy. "My uncle says

Henry may improve with time. You keep talking to him and loving him. He might fool us."

Mary used the summer to wean baby John, who was now a year and a half old. To be more accurate, John mostly weaned himself. He was so busy exploring the world around him and trying to keep up with his active brother that he basically forgot about nursing. By the end of the summer, he was weaned without any effort on Mary's part.

Over the summer, Mary managed to help some with food preservation for the winter – the shelling of beans and peas to dry, making kraut and pickles, and drying apples, but more often than not, Lucy would say, "You watch the babies; I'll help Emmie Lou." Fall would bring the making of cider and molasses, and preserving meat for the coming year, but the men folk would do the majority of that work. Cal, his brothers, several neighbors and a few slaves would work together on those tasks. What little remained of food preservation in the fall could be handled by Emmie Lou alone, giving Mary and Lucy time to focus on making clothes for the family.

As the first signs of fall began to appear, Mary remarked to Lucy about the coming anniversary of her arrival. "Can you believe it's been almost a year since you came here? It seems so recent."

"It's been the happiest year of my life, Miss Mary. I hate to think what might have happened if Mr. Cal hadn't rescued me. My babies would probably both be dead, and I might be, too."

"I understand why you think your babies might have died, but why do you think you might be dead too?"

"Because I probably would have used an iron skillet on that old drunk the first time he tried to rape me. Then I would have been tried for murder and hung." Lucy laughed in spite of the grim picture she had just painted.

"Well, that certainly isn't a very pretty picture, Lucy. I'm glad we kept you from coming to that end. Thank God Cal took a trip to Dandridge on that particular day."

"Yes Ma'am. Thank God he did!"

In late fall, Mary realized that she was pregnant again. She had been so busy with her lessons for the older children and the preparation of clothing for winter that she hadn't noticed the earliest signs of the pregnancy. As she thought back now to specific dates, she figured the baby would be due in late June or early July. She didn't worry too much about it, knowing that she would get a better estimate based on when she felt the baby move. She thought with relief that she wouldn't be going through the entire summer large with pregnancy.

Soon, Mary moved on to thinking about a name for another baby. She'd already named a daughter for her mother-in-law and grandmother, one son for her Uncle Samuel, and one son for her husband's father and her own father. If this baby was a boy, she wasn't sure what she would name it. She knew that Cal had said he didn't like the name Calvin and didn't want a son named Calvin. So, she wasn't sure what she would name the baby if it turned out to be a boy. She thought perhaps if the baby was a girl, she would name it for her Aunt Eliza and her sister Eliza, even though her sister had once demanded that she not ever do that.

The rest of Mary's pregnancy was uneventful. Cal doted on her as usual, and Lucy pampered her. Labor was short; Mary presumed because her body knew exactly what to do now, with this being her fourth baby. A beautiful and healthy Eliza Priscilla was born on June 25, 1851.

As Cal looked at his new daughter for the first time, he whispered to Mary, "Another miracle; another gift from God! You were my first gift. Now we have four more treasures."

"Cal, no matter how many babies we have, each one is so unique, so special from birth on. I think a lot of people believe all babies are alike, but they're not, not at all. Each baby has its own personality, its own way of interacting with the world from the time it's born."

"You have more opportunity to observe our babies at first, but I know they sure are fun to watch and talk with as they get older. They're so full of questions, so eager to learn. I had no idea being a father would be so much fun."

"Life seems pretty perfect; doesn't it?"

"Yes, it does, Mary, and I feel like I owe most of my happiness to you. These have been a wonderful nine years."

"Does it seem like that long to you?"

"Mostly no, but I guess the older you get, the faster time seems to pass. At least that's what my parents say. Dad is in his upper sixties now, and mother is sixty-five. They talk about time a lot, and I think Dad is worried about his health."

"Is it anything specific?"

"Not that I know of, but he's pretty stoic about things. I may be reading too much into it, but I see little things – like him trying to make sure each of his sons has some land and seeing that his will is updated."

Mary didn't think too much more about it. Her father-in-law looked healthy and continued to manage his farm as usual. Mary had other things on her mind. She was busy with the children. Sarah was now eight years old, Shields was five, and John a very energetic two and a half year old. It took pretty much all of Mary's time to tend to the needs of the older children and the newest member of the family. By early fall, she resumed the school lessons for Sarah and David and decided to include Shields also. Baby Eliza was a cheerful, easy to care for baby, and her nap time coincided with the afternoon lessons.

By Christmas, Eliza was pulling up to the side of her crib and trying to take steps while holding to the top rail. Mary told Cal, "I think Eliza is going to be an early walker. We're going to have our hands full then."

As Mary had predicted, by spring Eliza was walking and beginning to say a few words, although most of her vocabulary was a mystery. Although Mary had observed the development of her three older children, she was still filled with awe as she watched her youngest child develop into a very independent and eager to learn little individual.

In early May, Cal announced, "This year marks our ten year anniversary. We should do something special to mark the occasion."

"I don't know what you think we can do. I'm still nursing Eliza, so we can't very well go anywhere, but it is a nice thought."

"Well, I'm not giving up that easy. We could have a big party and invite my parents and all my brothers and their families and maybe some of the neighbors."

"That sounds like an awful lot of work, Cal."

"Don't worry about it. Emmie Lou and Lucy and I will take care of everything. Dad's right-hand man, Hamilton, can help me roast a whole pig, we can set up tables in the backyard, and everybody who comes can bring a dish or two of food. How does that sound?"

"It sounds like fun, and you're sweet to want to do it."

"Okay, just relax then. I'll handle everything."

May 26, 1852, dawned just as beautiful as the same date in 1842. As she dressed in the morning, Mary thought about her wedding day, the parlor filled with flowers, the guests and congratulations, and her eagerness to be Cal's bride. "I made a good choice," Mary said to herself. "Being married to Cal has been more wonderful than I could have imagined."

The picnic was wonderful. The yard was filled with family and friends, and the tables were laden with food. Uncle Samuel and Aunt Eliza were in attendance and brought Polly with them. Lucy looked after John and baby Eliza, leaving Mary free to mingle with the guests. Cal proposed a toast to "the most wonderful wife in the world," and Mary almost cried in spite of herself.

After the party was over and all of the guests had departed, Cal took Mary by the hand, saying, "Don't be in a hurry to go see about the little ones. They're fine. I want a few minutes alone with my wife." Cal took Mary by the hand, and without saying another word, led her in the door and up the stairs to their bedroom. He took Mary in his arms, kissed her passionately, and then said, "I love you so much that I don't have words to tell you. You're still just as desirable and even more beautiful than you were at eighteen when I so eagerly led you into this room to consummate our marriage. So, since I don't have enough words to express my love, maybe this little token will be a reminder of how much I love you."

Cal reached into his pocket and pulled out a small locket on a gold chain and fastened it around Mary's neck.

"Oh, Cal, it's beautiful, and I've never doubted your love. Later, I'll try to show you how much I appreciate that love."

With a twinkle in his eye, Cal asked, "I guess I have to wait until later to take you up on that offer?"

"Yes, later there won't be any chance of John knocking on the door and wanting to know why he can't come in or Eliza crying to be fed. So give me one more kiss and turn me loose. I'll see you at supper."

Chapter 11

Unto Everything a Season

Summer came with its usual scorching heat. Mary was grateful to not be pregnant this summer. She still remembered how miserable she had been prior to Sarah's August birth and Shields' July birth. She almost wished she wasn't still nursing little Eliza, but Eliza didn't seem ready to give up the breast. Also, Mary thought that her continued nursing of the baby might postpone another pregnancy. She loved each of her babies but didn't want to have babies at the rate her sister was having them. Mary laughed to herself, "I warned her when she married at sixteen that she might wind up with eleven or twelve children. At the rate she's producing babies, I almost think she's turning them over to a wet nurse. I'm not about to ask her though."

When the first cool mornings of late August arrived, Mary enjoyed feeling the breeze through the open window of the bedroom. She often paused to watch the cows in the field across the river and the morning mist rising from the river. She remembered how fearful she had been of the ferry at first. Now she thought nothing of it. She crossed it often to visit her in-laws and to attend church in New Market. The cool air reminded her that soon the trees would start to reveal their fall colors, red and gold everywhere like each tree was trying to outdo the one next to it. It was hard to know which was her favorite season, spring with its riotous explosion of blooms on the redbuds and dogwoods or fall with its glorious colors. "Well, she said to herself, "I don't really have to choose, do I? I can love them both, just like I love each of my children."

As the weather got cooler in late September and early October, Mary taught the children about the changing leaves and had them join her on the porch to watch the squirrels gather acorns to save for the winter. It was a different kind of school lesson, but one she and the children enjoyed. Mary also used this lesson to teach about the cycles of life, how plants that look dead in the fall, sleep over the winter, and come back in the spring. "Of course," she said, "we help some plants come back by saving their seeds to plant in the garden.

I can show you corn and beans and even tomato seeds that we've saved to plant next spring." Mary was pretty proud of herself. She had taught the children some important things, and they just thought they'd had a day off from school.

Late October arrived, and Mary was looking out the window at the leaves as she dressed early one morning when she noticed the ferry starting to cross from the other side. She couldn't help but wonder who was crossing so early in the morning. Most of the farmers around would be milking cows or having an early breakfast at this hour. "I'm too nosy," she thought, and dismissed the question from her mind. As she stepped into the next room to see if little Eliza was awake yet, she heard Cal come back into the bedroom.

Mary took one look at Cal's face and immediately knew something was wrong.

"Dad's dead."

"Oh, no! What happened?"

"Mother found him this morning when she went to see why he wasn't up and getting ready for breakfast. Apparently he just died quietly during the night. Went to sleep, and that was it. I guess it was his heart."

"Who was that who came to tell you?"

"It was Hamilton. He was bawling like a baby. He's known Dad all his life. I think his mother was a slave Dad inherited from his father."

"Do you think there's anything I can do for your mother right now?"

"I don't think so. Hamilton said somebody else was going for my sister. I think she'll be with Mother. One of my brothers was going over to New Market to get Mr. Minnis to send someone for the body. You and I can go over later, but I don't know when Minnis will bring the body back."

"Things are so different now. When Mama died twenty years ago, the neighbors came and prepared the body."

"You were just a little girl. How much of that do you remember?"

"All of it. I especially remember how heart broken Daddy was."

"He still is, isn't he?"

"Yes, I don't think that will ever change, Cal."

"Well, let's go have some breakfast. If Eliza is still asleep, just wake her up, change her and bring her with you. I'll see to getting the other children ready for breakfast…Oh, and I might as well tell you now. I've seen Dad's will, and I'll be inheriting several of his Negroes. I know you won't be happy about that, but you must have recognized that some of those folks have already been helping me put in and tend crops."

"Yes, Cal, I knew. I didn't think God had sent down some dark skinned angels to help in the fields."

"Then you surely understand that my hands are tied. I can't tell these folks to pack their bags and head north to Illinois or some other place where freed Negroes can live."

"Yes, I do understand. I still hate the very idea of slavery, but I do know what the manumission laws are."

The morning of the funeral dawned crisp but not unpleasantly cool. Mary left the two youngest children in Lucy's care so she and Cal could attend the funeral without lugging two little ones up the hill to the cemetery. She chose to include both Sarah and Shields because she knew they were fond of their grandfather, and she thought they deserved to see him laid to rest.

Once in the little cemetery, Mary breathed in the stillness. Even with the crowd of people, the hill was absolutely silent until the service started. Mary thought that even the cows in the field and the birds in the trees must think this was a holy place. As she waited for the service to begin, Mary recalled the first time she visited the cemetery. It was soon after she and Cal married, and she had remarked on the beauty of the field across the river from their home. Cal had invited her to walk up the hill with him, had shown her the graves of his grandparents, and shared how his dad had once brought him up the hill to show him those graves. Cal had told her how proud his dad was of his father's role in the Revolutionary War, especially the fact that he had been a captain in the battle of King's Mountain. Cal had pointed to the grave and relayed his memory of what his father had said. "I still remember how he said, 'This is our heritage, son. Don't ever forget it.' It was the first time I ever saw my dad with tears in his eyes."

Just before the minister began to speak, Mary looked around the little cemetery and thought again what a peaceful place it was. "Some day Cal and I will be laid to rest here also, and perhaps some of our children if they don't marry and move far away." The thought wasn't distressing. She just hoped she wouldn't be a widow for a long time if Cal should die first.

The minister read from the Bible, focusing on the passage from Ecclesiastes that speaks of a time to be born and a time to die. Then he talked about what a godly man John Nance, Jr. was and how he would be missed by his wife and children. After the closing prayer, neighbors started to leave and the pallbearers lowered the coffin into the grave. When that was done, Cal's mother kissed a fall flower she was carrying and dropped it onto the coffin. Then she turned to the family and said, "Please come by the house for a while. Neighbors have brought in a ton of food."

On the short walk to her in-laws house, Mary mentioned to Cal how she remembered the first time they had visited the cemetery together. "I remember how you recalled your memory of your father taking you to the cemetery and talking about your heritage. I don't remember though that you said much about your grandmother. I noticed today on the marker that she outlived your grandfather by several years."

"Yes, he died the year I was born, but Grandma Molly lived another six or seven years. Her name was Mary, but everybody called her Molly. She was quite a character. After my grandfather died, my Dad and Uncle Reubin didn't think Grandma Molly was making very wise decisions about some things. They went before a judge and asked that she be declared incompetent to handle her own affairs. She was furious, went before the same judge and convinced him that she had all her faculties. He rescinded his previous order. I don't think she did have all her faculties at that point, but fortunately, granddaddy's will was iron-clad enough that she couldn't make too much mess of things."

"Do you think your mother is going to be okay?"

"She's going to be lonely. That will be the main thing. Maybe she'll visit around with some of us grown children and do things like helping tend to newborns. She'll be welcome at our house, and we have a guest room."

During the meal with all of Cal's family, Mary was amazed at how the family, having just buried their patriarch, could come together with such a joyful air. They laughed, they told stories on each other, and they shared memories of childhood transgressions and the discipline meted out by their father. It was a different experience for Mary, but "Perhaps," she thought, "there is something very healing about family laughter in the face of death. Perhaps what I've observed today is a way of saying that what their father left lives on."

As Cal and Mary were about to leave the gathering, his mother said, "Wait, I have something for you." She left the room briefly and returned with something wrapped in a piece of linen. "Jackie wanted you to have this for John. It's the vest his father bought for him shortly before they moved from Virginia to Tennessee. It was made in North Carolina. I think before his father bought this property in Tennessee, he first looked at some land in North Carolina. He was familiar with that area because of his military service there. He probably bought a vest for Reubin, too, although I'm not certain. If Reubin passed one down in his family, it's likely long since worn out. This little vest has been in the cedar chest for years. You can see it's the right size for a ten or twelve year old boy. It'll be a few years before your little John can wear it, or you may never want him to wear it. Regardless, it's yours to keep for him."

"Are you sure this isn't something you want to hold onto, Mother? And why are you giving it to us today?"

"No, I do not want to hold onto it. Jackie said very specifically that he wanted his namesake to have it."

"My brother Noah has a son named John, also."

"It doesn't matter, Cal. He wanted your John to have it. So honor his wish, take the vest, and get out of here. You're too old to spank."

Mary was afraid Cal might be depressed after his father's death, but he didn't seem to be. Maybe he hugged her a little tighter and trotted children on his knee a little more often, but otherwise he seemed to be the same Cal. There were some legal matters to which he had to attend, but those didn't seem to bother him either.

The family settled back into their usual routines involving the farm and the children. Mary focused a lot of attention on lessons for the children. There might not be a school nearby, but Mary figured she might know as much or more than the average teacher anyway. She had read pretty much everything in her uncle's expansive library, including most of his medical books. Plus, no one could possibly care more about seeing that her children were educated than she did. One other advantage that Mary saw to educating the children at home was that they weren't constantly being exposed to the multitude of illnesses that ran rampant among groups if children.

The rest of that school year passed, and Mary began to think about starting separate classes over the summer for John and George to teach them their ABCs and how to print all the letters. John wouldn't be five until December, but he seemed bright, and it wouldn't hurt to get him off to an early start. George was nine months or so younger than John, but he and John were almost inseparable. Mary figured she might as well "kill two birds with one stone," so to speak.

She didn't know whether to try to include Henry in the lessons or not. She tended to think it would be better to wait until she was teaching Eliza to attempt to work with Henry. He did talk some, but his speech was so garbled it sounded like that of a two-year old. At least, he was finally potty trained and, according to Lucy, had learned to dress himself.

Mary decided there was plenty of time for those decisions later. Right now, it was time for Eliza's second birthday, and she had sent David over to ask her mother-in-law if she would like to come for supper and some cake.

Eliza was old enough now to realize that the celebration was about her and for her. She seemed to enjoy the entire celebration immensely.

After the celebration was over and Lucy had removed Eliza from the table for a face washing, Cal's mother asked if the rest of the children could be excused from the table also. She said she had something she wanted to discuss with just Cal and Mary. As soon as the children left the table, Cal's mother made her grand announcement.

"I wanted the two of you to be the first to know that I plan to remarry."

"Mother, are you out of your mind? Dad hasn't been gone a year yet. I never in a million years thought you'd remarry and certainly not this soon."

"I know this seems sudden to you, Cal. Please understand that my heart will always belong to your father. Nothing will ever change that."

"Then why are you planning to remarry, and who is it, pray tell?

"I'm lonely; simple as that. I can't abide being alone. I went from my father's house to a home with your father, and soon that home was filled with a passel of young'uns. Now there's just me."

"Mother, you're more than welcome to come live with us."

"No, my mind is made up. Jeremiah Jarnigan proposed marriage, and I said yes. He'll be good to me, provide well for me. He's lonely, too. We knew each other when we were young. He even courted me a little back then, but your daddy won my heart. Now, if you don't mind, I'd like to go home now. I'll have to go through this inquisition with each one of your siblings I guess."

"I'm sorry, Mother. I love you and want what's best for you, but this just seems sudden."

"Well, I think I know what's best for me, and I'm going home now."

When Cal's mother had left, Mary was the first to speak. "Cal, we didn't even ask when this wedding is to occur."

"It doesn't matter, Mary. She's stubborn as a mule. She's made up her mind she's going to do this, and she's going to do it regardless of what I or any of my siblings think."

"I'm sorry, Cal."

"Don't worry about it, Mary. Mother will get over being mad. I know her; she'll simmer down. We'll make up. I'll take my cue from her. She may never mention this discussion again. I'll just wait and see. Right now, I could use a hug from my wife, and then we need to see what birthday girl is up to."

Cal didn't see his mother again until he was summoned to the attorney's office for the final sign-off on the probate of the will and his mother's signing of a quit-claim on the property where she had lived. His mother was accompanied by Jeremiah Jarnigan and introduced herself to the attorney by her new name, indicating the marriage had taken place as planned. She was friendly to Cal, but much as he had suspected, made no mention of their animated discussion in the early summer.

In the fall, Mary focused a lot of her time on teaching her children as well as George and David. She was especially pleased to see that both George and David were very bright and eager learners. Phooey on the people who claim that people of the Negro race have inferior intellect!

It was just before Christmas that Mary began to suspect that she was pregnant again. She waited until Christmas day to tell Cal. While they were still in bed, Mary turned to Cal to say, "Before we go see if the children are anxious to open their presents, I have a present for you."

"That sounds like fun. Do we have time before the children start breaking down the door?"

"No, not that kind of present, Cal. Remember the first year we were married the gift I gave you on Christmas?"

"Yes, you told me you thought we were expecting a baby."

"Well, I know I can't expect you to be that excited again, but I think we are going to add number five to our little brood."

"When can we expect this little bundle?"

"Late August. I'll have the pleasure of being as big as a cow during the worst of the summer."

"Sorry about that, but I'm not sorry we're going to have another baby. Now let's get ourselves out of this bed and get downstairs. Eliza should really enjoy Christmas this year."

As with her other pregnancies, Mary's pregnancy progressed without problem. As the date neared for the baby's birth, Mary asked Cal for help in naming the baby.

"You've said every time that since I was the one giving birth, I should pick the name, but how about a little input from you?

"If it's a girl, we could name her Mary Elizabeth after my sister."

"That's fine with me, Cal, but please let's don't call her Mary or Lizzie. Can she just be Elizabeth?"

"Sure, that sounds good to me. My sister will be thrilled that we're naming a baby for her, but you'd better pick out a boy's name, too."

Mary thought the baby might arrive on Sarah Jane's birthday, August 28. Sarah was hoping that too, but little Mary Elizabeth didn't wait that long. She arrived in the world on August 16. Mary settled into the early days of frequent feedings and interrupted sleep. She determined that she would postpone the start of school lessons until at least the first of October and prayed that the baby would be sleeping through the night by that time. A couple of her babies had slept through the night early, and Mary recalled that it made a world of difference in how she felt. She guessed all mothers probably had the same wish. A baby crying during the night never seemed to bother Cal. He could sleep right through it. Of course, he could also sleep through all but the loudest of thunder storms.

Mary fell in love with this new baby, just as she had fallen in love with all her other babies. She stroked the soft skin, marveled at the precious little face, and tried to decide which of her other babies this baby most favored. She asked three year old Eliza who the baby looked like, and Eliza was quick to answer. "She looks like me, Mommy."

Mary thought Eliza might be jealous of the new baby, but that didn't seem to be the case. Instead, Eliza spent a lot of time watching her mother care for the newborn and tried to mimic the same actions with one of her dolls. She pretended to clean the doll's bottom, wrapped it in a blanket, and held it to her chest to nurse it. Mary thought Eliza's actions adorable.

After each birth, Mary wondered if their family was complete, but nature had other ideas. In 1856, Mary found herself pregnant for the sixth time. She secretly hoped for a boy this time but had another girl on November 3. She determined this baby would have an original name, not a name taken from some family member, so this baby was named Ellen Joannah.

Sarah, at age eleven, helped some with the care of the youngest members of the family, but more often it was little Eliza who played mother to her younger sisters.

Mary put school lessons on hold until after Christmas following little Ellen's birth. With so many children of different ages to teach, lessons took more of Mary's time, but she remained committed to seeing that all the children in the household were educated. The only child she hadn't been able to make much progress with was young Henry. Mary saw no hope in teaching him how to read. At seven, he couldn't say the alphabet or recognize any of the letters. On the other hand, he was a friendly, loving child and very compliant with simple directions. Mary thought that perhaps Henry would eventually be able to help with simple farm chores.

As the winter months passed and the first signs of spring emerged, Mary remarked once again to Cal how rapidly the years seemed to be passing. "I guess it's because I've been so busy, but it seems impossible that we will soon have been married fifteen years."

"Would you like another big picnic like we had to celebrate our tenth anniversary?"

"It's a sweet thought, Cal, but I think there are too many little ones under foot to even consider it. Let's just be grateful for all we have: six beautiful and healthy children, a deep love for each other, a prosperous farm, and more blessings than we can count."

"You're right, Mary. In fifteen years, the worst thing we've experienced is the death of my father."

"What about your mother's re-marriage?"

"That's her life. She doesn't seem to regret her decision, so who am I to say she was wrong? If marrying again keeps her from being lonely, maybe that's better than your heart-broken dad living all these years in his store since your mother died more than twenty-five years ago."

"That's true. He's seventy-one this year, but he's been a broken man ever since Mama died. That's a third of his life."

"Well, enough of this morbid talk, Mary. We started out talking about how blessed we are, and somehow we wound up talking about your father and his deep grief."

"You're right. Let's be thankful for what we have. These have been a blessed fifteen years, and I'm still grateful that you walked into my uncle's store on a day when I happened to be helping."

"I think you said that Doc Sam didn't much like you being in the store because of too much 'riff-raff' coming in."

"Well, you definitely did not fall in that group, and when you waved and said 'See you soon,' I was smitten."

"Still smitten?"

"Absolutely!"

Chapter 12

Broken Hearts

The summer of 1857 brought major changes to the household, beginning with a plea from Polly to Cal about the possibility of purchasing her from Doctor Sam. Cal had made a trip to Shields Station for supplies when Polly saw him arriving and came out into the yard for a private conversation.

As Cal reported the conversation to Mary later, Polly indicated her increasing frustration with the amount of work expected of her.

"I used to cook just for the family, but now I'm expected to prepare breakfast for overnight guests at the inn and lunch for stage coach passengers. Also, I'm frequently asked to prepare food to send over to the tavern in the evenings, and there's always some kind of party that Mrs. Shields is hosting. Maybe she's trying to get the girls married off; I don't know. I just know that I'm not as young as I used to be, and I was wondering if there is a chance you and the missus would see fit to try to buy me. According to a letter I got from Emmie Lou, Sibby has been writing her and begging her to come live with them. She says Luke has done well and could afford to pay you. Sibby thinks both Emmie Lou and David would fit right in, color wise, in their community and not have the stigma of being slaves. I could take over the cooking that Emmie Lou has been doing for your family."

"Polly, let me discuss this with Mary. I'd also like to have Luke's address so I can write him."

After discussing the situation with Mary and corresponding with Luke, Cal made the decision to make Doctor Sam an offer for Polly. Mary was still less than enthusiastic about purchasing a slave even though that person was Polly.

"Cal, I despise the whole idea of buying someone, but I do love Polly and want to do what's best for her. If she wants to join our household, then so be it. If Luke and Sibby are sure that Emmie Lou and David would fit right in with folks in their community, I'm all for that too. Emmie Lou has always been a little darker than Sibby, but she's still pretty light skinned, and David is probably at least three-quarters white. We know the man who fathered him was white…Do you think Uncle Samuel is likely to accept your offer?"

"I'll try to make it worth his while. I can't guarantee he'll accept, but I do know he's still trying to help John Howard finance his business in Knoxville."

An offer was made and accepted, and Polly came to join the household. Two days later, Luke came to escort Emmie Lou and David to Hancock County. Luke assured Polly that although he would have papers of ownership, Emmie Lou and David would live free. "No one in my community will have any idea that they are legally slaves."

Everyone seemed happy with the new arrangement. Polly was especially thrilled and let her pleasure be known. "You can't know how nice it is to be here, on this peaceful farm and away from that dusty road and all the suspicious looking characters traveling on it. I guess I never did trust anybody after that thug assaulted Emmie Lou. I didn't get to see Emmie Lou much after she moved here, and I haven't seen Sibby since she moved away. Still, I feel good knowing they're living free, and you're like another daughter to me, Mary. I still remember you, eight years old and missing your mama, climbing on my lap and asking if you could call me Aunt Polly. Plus, you never thought you were too good to help out in the garden or in the kitchen. You taught both Sibby and Emmie Lou how to read, and you were always Sibby's best friend. Heavens, you almost delivered David. Then Mr. Cal and you brought Emmie Lou and David here, gave them a safe place to live, and you taught David just like you were teaching your own children. Of course, I'm glad to be here."

"We're glad to have you here with us, Polly. I hope you can stand all the young'uns under foot. With Lucy's two and my six, it seems like there are always children about. As to my children, Sarah will soon be fourteen, Shields is already eleven, and John will be nine in December. They're not much trouble anymore. Even my Eliza, at age six, is quite the little mother to her two little sisters. She absolutely adores them. You also may see two other little fellows about some. They belong to Hamilton who came to us after Cal's father died. Their mother is dead, and I think Hamilton is trying to convince Lucy to marry him."

After Polly had been a part of the household for several weeks, Mary asked her about her workload. "Polly, are you sure we're not asking too much of you, cooking for this many people?"

"No, it's not too much. Lucy and her children have breakfast and supper at home. I just cook for them at lunch. You and Mr. Cal are satisfied with a simple menu, and you've taught your older children how to set the table, clear the table, and help with other kitchen chores. You even have somebody else tending the garden. My work here is nothing compared with what I was being expected to do at your uncle's place."

It was late August now, and Sarah asked if she could bake her own birthday cake. Polly said "Absolutely," and Sarah baked her own cake. Everyone in the entire family thought she had done a wonderful job and said so. By the time everyone had a piece, there was hardly a crumb left.

Later, Mary said to Cal, "You realize that our oldest child is turning into quite a young lady? She's only three years younger than I was when you proposed to me."

"That was yesterday, wasn't it?"

"You wish! You'd still be twenty-eight, and I'd still be a tiny little seventeen year old."

"You're still pretty tiny."

"Well, let's just say I'm proportioned a little different after six babies."

"Doesn't make any difference to me. You're still the girl I fell for, and I think you're proportioned just fine."

With the arrival of September, Mary began to think about lessons for the year. Lucy hadn't tried to attend the classes since the first year or two after her arrival, and the older children were so proficient at reading and basic math that Mary wasn't sure what she would be able to teach them this year. Maybe she could get Cal to check with her Uncle Samuel about some books on more advanced subjects. In the meantime, she could focus on getting Eliza off to a good start with her schooling and have some time to enjoy being a mother to her two youngest daughters. Little Elizabeth was four now and loved having stories read to her, and Ellen was only ten months old. That was quite enough to keep her busy. "Maybe, I'll even have a chance to enjoy the fall colors," Mary said to herself. "Last year I was too far along in my pregnancy to get out and enjoy the fall scenery much. I had the view from my bedroom window and from the porch, and that was about it."

On September 17, a rider came from Graham's Chapel with terrible news. There had been a fire and explosion at the store the previous night. The building was completely destroyed, and William Graham had perished in the fire. Cal was informed first and then broke the news to Mary. All she could do was cry and let Cal hold her in his arms. After a few minutes, she was able to ask about arrangements. Cal was firm. "Mary, I will ride over to Graham's Chapel for the service and to see if there are any immediate business details with which I need to be involved. You, however, are not going anywhere. It's too long a trip, and you need to be here with the baby. You daddy is at peace now, regardless of the cause of his death. Please try to remember that."

Mary didn't try to argue. In a sense, she was relieved that she didn't have to make the decision about trying to attend the service for her father. She hadn't been back to Graham's Chapel since she left as an eight year old child. She was glad that Cal was willing to go, but her baby was the one who needed her now, not her dead father.

Cal did ride over to Graham's Chapel later that day and was gone for three days. He stayed long enough to determine that the family living in the Graham home was not going to be displaced. William Graham had updated his will when he accepted responsibility for the family. Ownership of the family was to pass to a local minister William Graham respected with the stipulation that the family would be allowed to live on in the home, and in the case manumission laws were changed to allow freeing them, they would be given their freedom and ownership of the house. The minister had assured Cal that, for the time being, the father and older children could help tend to the church and church grounds and assist him in service to the community.

Mary was relieved to hear about these arrangements and took pleasure in knowing that her father, at heart, was a decent person, even if he hadn't been exactly the kind of father she would have liked.

The rest of 1857 and the first part of 1858 passed quickly. Schooling for the children proceeded as Mary had planned. The older children read as their primary means of learning while Mary worked with Eliza and Elizabeth.

During the winter months, the family generally did not try to make the trip to New Market to attend church. The size of the family required taking the wagon, and Mary didn't like the children having to ride so far exposed to the elements. Furthermore, the roads were often such a mess in the winter that they were almost impossible to travel with the wagon. When better weather came in the late spring, the family did try to attend church. Mary liked knowing that her children were in Sunday school with other children as well as getting to hear the minister's sermons.

It was mid-June when Mary heard the minister ask for prayer for two children in the church who were ill with diphtheria. Mary was frightened. She had read about the disease in one of her uncle's books although it had been called by a slightly different name. She knew the disease could have dire consequences, even be deadly. On the way home, she asked Cal if he had heard what the minister had said. Yes, he had heard, but he wasn't too worried, he told Mary.

"Our children are all healthy. They should be fine. You worry too much. Plus, didn't Sam vaccinate all our children?"

"Uncle Samuel vaccinated our children against smallpox. That has nothing to do with diphtheria. I don't think there is a way to prevent that."

Three days passed, and Mary began to relax. "Cal is probably right. I do worry about the children a lot, but I am their mother. That's my role, isn't it?"

Mary knew that one of the children the minister had mentioned was always a sickly looking child. Likely, his basic constitution made him prone to disease.

It was the next morning that Elizabeth came to Mary, complaining of a sore throat. "Mommy, my throat hurts."

"Open your mouth, and let me take a look."

The throat just looked a little red. Mary felt of Elizabeth's forehead. The child was definitely feverish, not real hot but warmer than she should be."

"Maybe it's just something simple," Mary told herself. "Let's find you something to drink. That might make your throat feel better." Mary took Elizabeth by the hand and led her out to the kitchen where Polly was preparing breakfast. "Polly, Elizabeth needs something to soothe her throat. Could we have a glass of milk, please?"

Milk in hand, Mary led Elizabeth out of the kitchen and to the back porch. "Now, sit here and sip the milk and see if that doesn't make your throat feel better."

Elizabeth tried to drink from the glass. "I can't swallow, Mommy. It really hurts." Then she threw up just as Lucy and her twins showed up.

"Lucy, keep your children back away from Elizabeth. Draw a bucket of water from the cistern to throw on this mess, please. Then just let the sun dry the spot. I'm going to take Elizabeth back to bed."

Fortunately, Mary had already weaned baby Ellen, so it was possible to turn her care over to Lucy for the most part while she tended to Elizabeth. Elizabeth took only sips of water during the entire day and continued to complain about her throat. Polly prepared some special broth for her, but she couldn't take any of that either.

Mary was increasingly concerned. She thought the throat looked worse by late in the evening and asked Cal if either he or Hamilton could ride over to Shields Station early the following morning to see if Doctor Sam could come.

Mary rested but little that night, getting up often to check on Elizabeth who was sleeping but had thrown off all the covers. In the morning, when Mary looked at Elizabeth, she was shocked at how much sicker she appeared. Her skin was dry, her voice was a whisper, and she was definitely more feverish than on the previous day. Mary could do little except bathe her child's face with a wet cloth and hold her in her arms.

Doctor Sam showed up about noon and confirmed Mary's worst fears. Elizabeth had all the symptoms of diphtheria and was beginning to form the tell-tale greyish membrane on the throat.

"Mary, by all means, keep the other children away from this child. I know you have one who is only about eighteen months or so, and she is going to want her mother. Nevertheless, you need to stay away from her because you've been in direct contact with this very sick child. Do continue to try to get this little one to take some fluids. If she can't take fluids by mouth, we will have to resort to a rubber feeding tube which she will hate, or fluids through the rectum. Of course she won't like that either, but dehydration is very dangerous to a child."

"Is there anything else I can do, Uncle Samuel?"

"I wish there were, my dear, but it's mostly in God's hands. Medicine has little to offer."

Later that day, Lucy reported that Henry was also ill. That meant she had to stay home to care for him. Sarah took over care for baby Ellen, and Eliza appointed herself "guardian of the gateway" to the sickroom, making sure that none of her siblings tried to bother Mary and her little sister.

For ten days, Mary did everything she could for Elizabeth, but the disease won the battle. Little Elizabeth died on June 26, the day after Eliza's seventh birthday. Doctor Sam said it was likely that her heart just stopped.

Mary bathed the body of her precious child one last time and combed her hair. The funeral people in New Market delivered a small casket, but left preparation of the body to the family. They were too afraid of the disease to touch the body.

Cal's mother and sister came and scrubbed the sick room and everywhere they thought Elizabeth might have been before she showed symptoms. They opened the windows and mopped the floors twice. They burned the straw ticking mattress from Elizabeth's bed and washed the sheets and coverlet in the big iron kettle with boiling water and lye soap. It was all they could do.

On the day of Elizabeth's funeral, Mary crossed the river on the ferry and trudged up the hill to the little cemetery with Cal's arm supporting her about the waist. She stood at the graveside and heard the minister but remembered not one word he said. She did recall that a lady from their church sang "Shall We Gather at the River." Mary had never heard the song before. The lady later told her that she had recently visited in Brooklyn and a Baptist pastor there had recently written part of the song. It hadn't been published yet, but she had been so taken with it, she had written down the words and committed the melody to memory.

When she got home, Mary wanted to just go in her room and shut the door, but she was greeted by little Ellen who ran with outstretched arms to hug her mother. It was the first time in almost two weeks that she had been allowed to touch her mother. As Mary enfolded little Ellen in her arms, she was reminded of the words of her Grandmother Jane to Aunt Eliza all those years ago. "You must not let this loss consume the rest of your life. Remember you have five healthy children." Her grandmother had buried at least two of her own children by that time, including Mary's own mother. "I have no choice," thought Mary. "I have to try to pull myself together. I wish I could remember what else Grandma said…something about being thankful for the day God had made." She picked up little Ellen, kissed her, and hugged her tight.

The next day, Lucy came to say that Henry had died also. Mary wanted to hug Lucy, but she knew Lucy was probably still wearing the same clothes she had worn while caring for Henry. "I want to wrap my arms around you, Lucy, but I can't right now. Please understand. This disease seems to be so contagious, and I can't bear for any more of my children to get it."

"I understand, Miss Mary. I just wanted you to know."

"What about arrangements, Lucy? We can get a casket from Mr. Minnis in New Market and have a grave dug up on the hill if you'd like."

"No, ma'am. Hamilton says there's a cemetery close to New Market that's for people of color. His first wife is buried there. We'll put Henry there.

Hamilton says too that there's a slave in Mossy Creek who's a preacher. He's gonna see if he'll come say some words."

"Is George okay?"

"Yes ma'am. He seems fine. Of course, I've been holding my breath."

"Me too, Lucy. Me too. I keep trying to focus on what my grandmother said about remembering the other children."

"That's true, Miss Mary, and I keep thinking too about the fact that Henry weren't never gonna be right. You know that. Now he can be just like all the healthy children in Heaven. I don't reckon Heaven's got any not quite right young'uns."

It was a struggle for Mary to get through the next few months, but gradually time eased the intensity of her grief. She tried hard to focus on the needs of her other children, especially Eliza who had doted on both of her little sisters from the time they were born. Mary was able to lose herself some in the pleasure of seeing little Ellen's rapid transformation from infant into toddler and over and over reminded herself of her grandmother's words.

One thing that did continue to nag at Mary and intensify her grief was that Cal seemed withdrawn in the months following Elizabeth's death. Mary needed the comfort of Cal's arms, but he seemed withdrawn. Cal's expression of grief seemed to be the diametrical opposite of Mary's grief. His lack of any display of physical affection was so unlike him that Mary even wondered if it was his age, but she finally decided that what she was seeing was just Cal's response to the death of their child. Mary wanted to be able to talk to Cal but didn't know what to say. So she just hugged little Ellen close and let that suffice for the closeness she desired with Cal.

Little was done to celebrate Ellen's second birthday in November. Sarah baked a cake for her little sister, and Eliza sang a song for her. There were no gifts purchased and no fanfare.

As Christmas approached, Cal asked Mary what she would like for Christmas. She finally got up her nerve to speak her mind. "I want my husband back, Cal."

"What do you mean, Mary? I haven't gone anywhere."

"I want all of you back, Cal. It's been months since you touched me. I need you. I need the comfort of being in your arms. Do you at all understand what I'm saying?"

"I'm sorry, Mary. I hear what you're saying. I guess Elizabeth's death has been eating away at me. I know it isn't logical at all, but I feel like I should have been able to protect my family."

"You're right, Cal. That isn't logical or possible. I don't know why our child died, but I've gotten through these last few months by remembering what my grandmother Shields told Aunt Eliza after she lost twins. She said, 'Don't let this consume the rest of your life,' and then she challenged her to get about the business of living, really living. I guess I felt abandoned when my mother died and abandoned by my father who sent me away. Now, I feel abandoned by you too."

"If you're through preaching at me, could I have a hug now?"

"Yes, you may, sir," answered Mary as she stepped to wrap Cal in her arms.

That night Cal did his best to show Mary that she had not been abandoned.

Chapter 13

An Uncertain Future

As 1859 dawned, Mary could only pray that it would be a better year than the last two. The year 1857 had brought the loss of her father in the horrible fire, and 1858 had brought the death of precious little Elizabeth. Mary thought of that precious little child, always smiling and laughing, and so bright and pretty. Somehow, it still just didn't seem fair that a child with such promise had been taken. Sometimes now, as she looked out the window of her bedroom, the barrenness of the winter field across the river reminded her of how she still felt at times. She had once enjoyed looking across the river at that field and thought it looked beautiful in all seasons. Now, it was a reminder of a tiny grave in the cemetery at the top. She wondered if she would ever stop grieving for the loss.

The coming of spring did seem to lift Mary's spirits. Perhaps it was the renewal of life in the trees and plants. Perhaps it was just the passage of time.

Regardless, she did feel more human and more ready to follow the advice of Grandmother Jane.

Late in spring, a letter from Mary's sister mentioned that she would like to have a party in the early summer to celebrate Sarah's upcoming sixteenth birthday. She wanted to have the party before the arrival of the worst of the summer heat.

Mary laughed to herself. Her sister seemed to be following in the footsteps of their Aunt Priscilla. Mary remembered well the outcome of Aunt Priscilla's party where her sister Eliza met her future husband. She hoped that her sister wasn't plotting to marry off Sarah.

After several letters back and forth, Mary agreed to let Sarah go for a visit with her aunt. Just because she was still morose at times didn't mean Sarah shouldn't be allowed to experience some youthful gaiety.

In late May, Sarah went for a two week visit with her Aunt Eliza's family. When she returned, she was very excited and eager to share the memories of her visit. "Mother, it was so much fun. Aunt Eliza hosted a party while I was there, and I met the nicest young man."

"Uh-oh! That sounds serious. I hope you remember that you're still just fifteen. I don't want to see you married at sixteen like my sister."

"Don't jump to conclusions, Mother. I just said he was nice. He may not be remotely interested in me."

"Well, tell me about him. What's he like?"

"His name is Marshall Hughes. I think he's three or four years older than me. He's already working at a newspaper in Knoxville. I think his newspaper runs ads for Uncle Milton's business, or maybe his family has some tie to Uncle Frank. I didn't find out about that."

"Well, he sounds respectable enough, but I wouldn't expect my sister to invite any other kind of people to one of her parties. Is there anything else you need to tell me?"

"Not really, Mother. We just chatted for a while at the party. He was very polite and seemed very concerned when I happened to mention little Elizabeth."

"I'm glad you had a good time. Not much has happened here while you've been gone. I am feeling better than I've felt in months. The coming of spring brightened my spirits quite a lot, and I can't help but laugh at some of little Ellen's antics. She's growing and changing so fast. It seems like she's using new words by the dozens every day. She reminds me of what you were like at two and a half."

"You've had so many of us, Mother. I'm surprised you remember what I was like."

"Of course I remember what you were like, Sarah. You were my first born and so much fun to watch. Just like Ellen, you were talking a mile a minute at two and a half and had your daddy absolutely wrapped around your little finger. Some young man is going to have to be really something to convince your daddy he's good enough for you."

"Now you're the one trying to see into the future, Mother."

"Sorry! Guess I am. Anyway, I'm glad you had a good time at Eliza's. It's good to have you home though."

A few weeks later, Mary received a letter from her sister relaying a request from a young Mr. Hughes to initiate correspondence with Sarah. Eliza said in the letter that the young man was smart enough to figure out Sarah's rural address, but he didn't want to be presumptuous. He would not write unless Sarah was willing to receive his correspondence.

Cal and Mary gave their permission, and Mary relayed the information in a letter to her sister. Within a couple of weeks, the first letter arrived from Marshall Hughes. He expressed his delight in having received permission to initiate correspondence and noted that he hoped they would be able to meet again in the near future. After that, letters started arriving for Sarah on a weekly basis. As Sarah's August birthday approached, she began to hint to her mother that she would like to have her friend invited to help celebrate her sixteenth birthday.

Mary discussed Sarah's request with Cal, and it was the two of them who extended the invitation for a visit. Sarah's beau (at least it appeared he was a beau) wrote that he would be "most pleased to accept" their kind invitation. He would schedule his visit so that it did not interfere with his job at the newspaper.

Marshall Hughes did come for a three day visit and proved to be a very pleasant young man. After the visit, Sarah accused her father of having monopolized her friend's time, questioning him about what he was hearing at the newspaper about turmoil on the national scene. Cal had heard rumors that huge conflicts were brewing in Washington over the issue of slavery, so he had a good excuse to offer to Sarah. "I just thought Marshall Hughes might have a good idea of what's going on."

Weekly letters continued to be exchanged between Sarah and Marshall Hughes, and he began to mention that he hoped he would be invited for another visit at Christmas if weather permitted travel. Sarah relayed the question to her mother who said, "Yes, why not, but I don't think your father and I need to extend a formal invitation this time. Just tell Marshall we said he's most welcome to come for a visit."

Marshall Hughes did come for a visit at Christmas, and Mary thought it was the best Christmas the family had experienced in several years. The depressive cloud which had hung over the household for months after Elizabeth's death seemed to have finally lifted. Neither she nor Cal seemed to be depressed now, and their marriage again provided the affectionate interaction which was a sustaining force in Mary's life.

When New Year 1860 arrived, Mary thought back to the prayer she had said at the beginning of 1859. "It was a good year," she said to herself. "May the coming year also prove to be a good year."

Mary's hopes for a good year were soon dashed. In early January, both Shields and Eliza complained of sore throats. Mary was immediately worried. She hadn't heard of any cases of diphtheria since the summer Elizabeth died, but any sore throat frightened her anyway. Mary looked at the children's throats. They were red and swollen, but they did not look like little Elizabeth's throat had looked. Moreover, both Shields and Eliza were able to continue taking some fluids and nourishment and seemed to especially appreciate the soup Polly made.

Mary's fears were partially assuaged but not completely relieved. She noted that Shields seemed to have more problems breathing than Eliza and generally appeared sicker. When the children did not seem to be improving after a couple of days, Mary asked Cal if he would ask Hamilton or one of the other younger men on the farm to ride over to Shields Station and see if her uncle would come.

When Doctor Sam came and examined the children, he advised continued rest in a warm room, nourishment as tolerated, and salt water gargles. "I do not believe in bleeding with leeches, purges, or some of the strange medicines offered by some doctors in these cases. I believe that nature may be the best healer. Some of my colleagues need to remember that they took an oath to first do no harm. Or maybe some of these quacks who never had any real medical education other than to follow some other uneducated fellow around for a few weeks never took that oath. Regardless, just keep doing what you're doing for these children. I'll return in a few days and check on them."

After a few days, both children complained less with their throats, and Doctor Sam said the throats definitely looked better. There were other troubling symptoms, however, which were very worrisome. Both children complained that their joints hurt, and Shields had poor color and continued to experience a general weakness. Doctor Sam gave Mary some salicylate to administer for the joint pain and recommended continued rest for both children.

On his visit a week later, Doctor Sam told Cal and Mary that he very much feared that both children were suffering from Acute Rheumatism* with Shields' symptoms suspicious of his heart being involved. He could hear a murmur which was worrisome. He said he couldn't predict long term outcome.

When Cal pressed Doctor Sam for more information, he seemed hesitant to answer. After Sam left, Mary told Cal, "I think he's trying to protect us. I don't think he wants us to know how sick our boy is, but I'm not blind. I can see how sick he is. I wish

*Rheumatic Fever

I could remember if I ever read about this in one of Uncle Samuel's medical books, but I can't remember it. It might just scare me anyway."

Eliza apparently escaped the heart damage, but she soon developed nodules on her elbows and hands and complained of her knees hurting. Sometimes her legs and arms jerked involuntarily.

Doctor Sam explained that although the symptoms were very different in the two children, both illnesses started from their sore throats. He suggested rubbing Eliza's joints with some liniment he provided followed by wrapping the joints in warm flannel or woolen cloth. He did hold out hope that Eliza would eventually recover completely.

It was her uncle's failure to mention recovery for Shields that led Mary to conclude that Shields might never fully recover. Mary confessed to Cal that she felt completely helpless. "We were so lucky for so many years, Cal. All our children were bright, healthy, and such a joy to our lives. Then we lost our little Elizabeth and now this. I feel so completely helpless, and I don't know if I'm strong enough to deal with all that is happening now."

"Mary, it's my turn now to remind you of the need to draw strength from each other. We will get through this, together. Sam says he thinks Eliza is likely to recover completely, and he hasn't said that Shields won't recover. We have to hold onto that hope. In the meantime, you need to let Lucy handle more of the massaging and wrapping of Eliza's joints. You can't do everything yourself. Spring is coming, and when the weather gets really nice, we can see about taking Eliza to Tate Springs for treatment in the mineral waters. Sam says they have a good treatment program there."

Mary was so concerned about the health of her children that she was scarcely aware of the concern Cal had about the rising turmoil on the national scene. It wasn't until Marshall Hughes came for a visit in the spring that Mary realized there was talk of Tennessee seceding from the union to join with other southern states in something called the Confederate States of America.

When Mary asked Cal about what she had overheard in the conversation, he replied that it was all but a done deal. "Several states have already declared their independence from the union, and there will soon be a vote here on the matter. Lots of folks in middle and west Tennessee are strongly in favor of Tennessee's secession. More folks in east Tennessee are opposed."

"What do you think, Cal?"

"I think my granddaddy who fought in the revolution would turn over in his grave if he thought the union was going to be ripped apart."

"What about Sarah's friend? What does he think?"

"The editor of the newspaper where he works is strongly in favor of the Confederacy. To keep his job, Marshall has no choice but to keep his mouth shut and just print what he's told to print."

"What about my Uncle Samuel? Do you know what he thinks?"

"He had two grandfathers who fought in the revolution, Mary. I believe he thinks the same way I do. However, he advised me recently to keep my opinion to myself. He specifically said, 'Boy, the fewer people who know what you believe, the better. Just keep your mouth shut.' I think that's sound advice, and if anyone should ask you about my beliefs, just plead ignorance."

"Who would ask me about what you believe?"

"Your sister for one. Her husband and his entire family are pro Confederate."

"Do you have any idea why?"

"Follow the money. He's a business man and probably figures there's money to be made. I don't know for sure and don't intend to ask."

"With all these southern states voting to withdraw from the union, what's going to happen?"

"I can't foresee the future, but I can't believe that the U.S. government will take kindly to the entire southern half of the nation trying to form a different country. I think there'll be war."

"Oh, Cal, that's so scary."

"I know, Mary; I don't believe that a lot of folks are thinking about long term consequences of their actions. There's a lot of hullabaloo about states' rights, but I think it all boils down to the issue of slavery. A lot of wealthy people have gained their wealth by having large numbers of slaves work their plantations. That's why so many people in middle and west Tennessee want to join the Confederacy – so they can continue to prosper from slave labor."

"Cal, we have slaves, too. Are we blameless?"

"Yes, we do have a few slaves, but you know as well as I do that since the 1830s, the law here has required any slave being freed to leave the state within a year. Furthermore, manumission has been completely illegal since 1854. Polly is here by choice, and Lucy still thinks that coming here is the best thing that has ever happened to her. As to the slaves I inherited, I'd be happy to have them live free and earn a salary for their labor. That just isn't possible. Maybe someday, but not now."

"I know; we've had this conversation before."

As predicted by Cal, the secessionists won the vote in Tennessee. At the urging of Governor Harris, the state legislature voted on May 6, 1860, to become an independent state and to form an army of 55,000 men to support the cause of the Confederacy. A general referendum soon followed. The move into the Confederacy was underway. Cal knew that many people would assume he was pro Confederacy because he was both a slave owner and one of the wealthiest men in the county. He kept his mouth shut and let people think what they wanted.

After receipt of the news about secession, Mary asked Cal if he thought they would still be able to take Eliza to Tate Springs in the summer for treatment. The bad spasms in her legs were continuing.

Cal's response offered some sense of relief. "I don't think war is imminent, so I think we can still plan on doing that, Mary. I'll send a letter asking when we might be able to bring her. I do think you should let Lucy go along and learn the exercises or whatever they recommend while you stay here with Shields and the other children."

"Good, I'll talk with Lucy about that anyway. George can stay here. He and John are pretty much inseparable anyway."

Eliza did go for treatment during the latter part of the summer and seemed somewhat improved by the exercises and massages of her limbs. These procedures were attended to religiously by Lucy after their return home.

Mary wished there were some place Shields could be sent for treatment that would be equally helpful, but she had to accept that no such option existed. Shields remained frail and unable to tolerate any exertion.

Sarah's friend Marshall Hughes continued to visit about once a month but seemed to be in no hurry to take their romance any further than its status for the last year. Mary didn't know if the young man was hesitant to pursue a more permanent relationship due to the pending war or if Cal had perhaps suggested that he cool his ardor for a while.

As summer turned into fall and the end of the year loomed, Mary thought about the optimism she had felt at the beginning of the year. "I wonder if I'll ever again look upon a new year with such optimism?" she asked herself. "It's hard to believe that I will. I was just beginning to feel like myself again when the illness struck Shields and Eliza."

Regardless of Mary's outlook, the first of a new year did arrive. Christmas had been quiet, a small gift for each of the children and something a little extra for Ellen. Neither Christmas nor the coming of a new year was cause for celebration. January was bitter cold, and both Mary and Lucy focused on keeping fires going in the fireplaces so the rooms where Shields and Eliza slept would be warm enough for them. Mary decided to move Shields to the downstairs bedroom, believing it was a warmer room than upstairs and to keep him from having to climb steps.

A bit of relief from the cold weather came in mid-February, and Doctor Sam took that opportunity to ride over to see the children. During his visit, he mentioned that there had been some cases of diphtheria recently and he had been called to attend to a couple of children.

Four days after Doctor Sam's visit, Ellen complained to her mother that her throat hurt. "Mommy, my throat hurts," she squeaked out in a voice that sounded like she could barely speak. Mary responded with "Open your mouth, and let me take a look," while saying to herself, "Oh, please, oh God, don't let this be happening again!"

But Ellen was sick, and she soon began to show the symptoms of diphtheria, those symptoms with which Mary was all too familiar. Ellen was feverish, her throat formed the grey membrane, and it was almost impossible for her to swallow any fluids. In spite of Mary's diligent care and almost two weeks of sleepless nights as she sat with the child, little Ellen drew her last breath on March 4. Again, Mary bathed the little body, the body of a child she had brought into the world, combed her hair, and dressed her in her prettiest dress. Hamilton was sent to get a small casket from Mr. Minnis in New Market.

When Eliza learned of her little sister's death, she came bringing her favorite doll to her mother. "Please put this in the casket with Ellen. I'll never play with it again, Mother. My childhood is over."

Hamilton asked to dig the grave. The next day, the small casket was carried by Hamilton, George, and John down to the river as Cal walked along with Mary. A brisk wind blew as the little group crossed the river on the ferry, a reminder that winter wasn't over. The wind seemed to blow colder as they walked up the hill. Mary shivered although bundled in her woolen coat. She wasn't sure if she was shivering from the wind or from the grief shaking her to her core. The latter seemed more likely. Their Presbyterian minister from New Market said a few words and closed with a short prayer. No one else attended the funeral. Hamilton and George stayed behind to fill in the grave.

By the time the little party of three returned to the house, Mary was shaking uncontrollably. Lucy heated a blanket by the fireplace and wrapped it around Mary, but the shaking did not abate. All Mary could think about was how little Ellen had come running with outstretched arms after the service for Mary Elizabeth.

Mary excused herself from everyone else and retreated to her bedroom. She sat down in the rocker where she had rocked her babies literally hundreds of times, and hugging her arms about herself, she rocked back and forth as she cried and cried. She didn't know how long she sat in the chair rocking and crying, but eventually the dimming light in the room indicated she had been there for hours. It dawned on her that Cal was somewhere in the house, hurting also. She got up, washed her face in the basin, and went to look for Cal.

Chapter 14

Facing the Whatevers

Mary found Cal sitting by himself in the dim light of the parlor. "Cal, I'm so sorry I've behaved so badly this afternoon; I should have thought about the fact that you were hurting too. Instead, I went off by myself and cried myself empty."

"It's okay, Mary. I thought you needed to be alone for a little while. I just hope that you won't do like I did after Elizabeth's death. Don't shut yourself off from me. I think we need each other more than ever now. Remember we will see our babies again, and for now, we can take comfort in the fact that they never have to suffer again. To be alive means we have to suffer from time to time. It's as simple as that. We don't know what the future holds, but we have each other. We will face all the 'whatevers' together. Now, please hug me, Mary, and then we need to go to the dining room. Polly has prepared a little supper for us. She was here a few minutes ago to tell me that. The children have already eaten, and Lucy has gone home."

The days and weeks that followed were difficult. Mary spent her days trying her best to focus on caring for her family. Eliza's schooling had stopped over a year prior when she became ill, and Hamilton's two children also needed to be taught to read. Mary forced herself to resume teaching. She thought the children deserved no less. Four weeks after Ellen's death, Mary was in the middle of a lesson with the children when Lucy came to tell her that she had a visitor waiting in the parlor.

In the parlor, Mary found Bertha Broggins seated on the sofa. Mary took a seat across from her visitor as she spoke. "It's been a while since I've seen you, Bertha."

"Well, my dear, I've wanted to come ever since I heard about another of your little ones being taken. I do hope you will forgive me for not coming sooner. So many people have been visited with the sadness, and I felt it my duty to visit each one of those homes and bring what cheer I could."

"Cheer, indeed," thought Mary. "I've never known this woman to dispense anything remotely resembling cheer." Biting her tongue, Mary responded, "That must have kept you very busy indeed."

Bertha beamed. "Oh yes, my dear, but I do so want to comfort those whose families have suffered such terribly grievous events...those who have felt the hand of God reach right into the bosom of their family and snatch away one of their dear members. I, myself, have been so fortunate. That is, Mr. Broggins and I. Why none of ours have had as much as a sniffle during this most recent pestilence nor the one that took your other little girl."

Bertha babbled on, oblivious to the fact that Mary's face was unsmiling and her eyes glaring. "I often say to myself, 'Bertha Broggins, you have been so blessed by the Lord. Surely the good heath of your children is a reward for your good deeds.' Don't you agree?"

The last statement was more than Mary could stand and remain cordial. "That is indeed hard to understand, Bertha. What I hear you saying is that God himself caused my babies to suffer. That he reached down, made them sick, and then took them away from me because I haven't done enough good deeds…Now, let me be perfectly clear. I don't believe that. The God I worship does not torture innocent babies and precious children and snatch them away leaving broken hearted mothers behind. Now, if you don't mind, I have chores to do, and perhaps you have somewhere else you'd like to go share your favored status with God."

Mary rose from her chair and left Bertha, her face flushing red, to find her own way out.

Later that day, Mary confessed to Cal about her response to Bertha. "I probably shouldn't have responded to that woman that way, but she just got under my skin. I don't believe God singles people out to suffer, especially not innocent little children. He gives us strength to endure, but he does not select people to experience bad things. There are a lot of diseases that we don't understand. Even the doctors don't know what causes them. On the other hand, doctors now know how to prevent smallpox, and sometime in the future, they'll likely figure out a way to prevent or treat things like diphtheria and this disease that has sickened Shields and Eliza."

That weekend, Marshall Hughes came to visit Sarah and brought the latest news on the prospect of war. He said that lots of people in Knoxville seemed giddy over the prospect of war, and that Confederate flags were flying up and down Gay Street. Scores of young men were leaving to join the Confederate army. Others were fleeing to Kentucky to join the union forces. The only reason he wasn't being conscripted was because his job was considered essential at the newspaper, and his newspaper was pro Confederacy. He also reported that each state was beginning to print its own money, not backed by bank holdings but by a promise to pay the bearer of the note six months after the end of the war and signing of a truce.

When they were alone, Mary asked Cal what he thought about states printing their own money. "Marshall said states were printing money not backed by bank holdings. What do make of that?"

"The presumption is that the Confederacy will be victorious in a war with the federal forces. If the federal forces are the victors, that money printed by the states will have absolutely no value. It looks like I'll have to convert some money into Confederate bills just to be able to do business, but I intend to limit as much as possible my financial investment into this venture. This is a good time to tell you that ever since I heard the news of a possible war, I have quietly been putting as much money as possible into silver and gold."

"May I ask, pray tell, what you've been doing with the silver and gold you've acquired?"

"I should have already told you, but there has been so much else going on. I've divided the money out into several earthenware crocks with lids that I've sealed with wax. I buried one of them beneath one of the bee hives, one under blackberry briars at the edge of the pasture, and one in the ground under a cow patty in the barn. I'm changing out the cow patty every few days to keep it fresh. One day when you're feeling like it, I can take you around and show you all of these places. If war comes, this is going to be the best kind of money to have, regardless of the outcome of the war."

Shortly after Marshall Hughes visit, Mary told Cal that she had received a letter from her sister saying that her sons William and Samuel had both joined the

Second Tennessee Confederate Cavalry and had left for Virginia. "I have written her back saying I will pray for their safe return."

"Do you think she is worried about them?"

"Probably some. What mother wouldn't be? On the other hand, I think she's of the opinion that this war won't last long and will easily be won by the Confederacy."

"That's what a lot of people think, Mary, but I don't think most of them have any idea what war is really like. Of course I don't have any personal experience with war, but my father passed on some of the stories my grandfather shared about the Revolutionary War. No war is some little Sunday afternoon picnic as some people seem to think this war will be. Hundreds, probably thousands, of soldiers will die and perhaps some civilians also."

"I'm scared, Cal. Do you think the war could come here?"

"It could. We're not that far from the railroad running north and south. That railroad is going to be a major supply route, and both armies will be trying to control supply routes."

"I hadn't thought of that. Now, I'm more frightened."

"I didn't mean to scare you, Mary. Maybe I've told you more than I should have."

"No, you were just being honest, and I appreciate that. Like you said a few weeks ago, we'll face the 'whatevers' together."

As summer progressed, Cal and Mary received most of their news about the war from Marshall Hughes. All of the early battles seemed to heavily favor the Confederacy. The Confederates were clearly the victors at the first major battle, the August 28-29 battle at Manassas, Virginia. By September, there were several battles in West Virginia. Soon, they heard of battles in other places like Kentucky and Missouri. The news of these early Confederate victories led supporters of the Confederacy to believe that complete victory would soon come.

Some of the most alarming reports to reach Cal and Mary during the early part of the war were the accounts of roaming bushwhackers who preyed on private citizens. Some claimed to be unionists while others claimed an allegiance to the Confederacy. Regardless of claimed allegiance, all of the bushwhackers were lawless men who appeared to mostly want to plunder, stealing whatever they could get their hands on and not caring if they caused loss of life.

As these reports became more numerous, Mary's Uncle Samuel told Cal he was constructing a secret room in his house, a room that would shave off a few feet along one side of the inn and be accessible only through a closet in a bedroom of the family quarters. Doctor Shields suggested that Cal do something similar at his house.

Cal told Mary about her uncle's suggestion but puzzled over how he could accomplish such. "Mary, your uncle's plan for a hiding place makes sense for Shields Station, but that house already has fourteen rooms. There's no place in this house where I could construct a room that would be hidden. His room is going to be accessible through a closet. We have only one closet in the entire house, the one in our bedroom. The other bedrooms have wardrobes. There's no place for a room next to our closet."

The very next day, Cal announced to Mary that he had thought of an idea for a hiding place. It wouldn't be like her uncle's entire room, but it would be a hiding place.

"Mary, I've thought some more about what Sam said. There's no place I can put an entire room, but there is a hidden space in the wall behind our closet where the back stairs extend up to the attic. It isn't a very big space, probably only big enough for two people, but it is a space. I can split the beadboard on the back wall of the closet all the way across and cover the split with a piece of half-round trim. The top part will be attached with hinges to the edge of the flooring above. The hinged wall can be closed from inside with a simple hook. There will be a trap door in the attic for an exit, but we can place a heavy trunk on top of that. I'll get started on the construction this afternoon. John can help me."

As news of the war continued and larger and larger numbers of men were lost in battle, Mary took comfort in the fact that John wasn't old enough to be conscripted into the army. She tried to focus on what they had instead of what they had lost. Sarah and John were healthy, Eliza seemed to be slowly improving, and Shields appeared no worse. The farm itself remained productive and provided for virtually all their needs. Except for coffee, sugar, oil for the lamps, and fabric for clothing, almost nothing had to be purchased at the store. In most ways, life on the farm remained unchanged. Crops were planted, tended, and harvested. Animals were raised for food and to be sold. A large garden provided fresh produce all summer and food to be stored for the winter. Sometimes, it was difficult to remember that battles were raging elsewhere.

Cal remained convinced that the war would eventually come closer to them. "We live too close to the railroad, too close to the other major north-south routes through the valley for the war not to arrive on our doorstep sooner or later," he told Mary. "Maybe it will end before then," was Mary's reply.

"Maybe, but it doesn't look that way to me. The north has a lot of resources and a large army. President Lincoln appears to be looking for the right generals to lead that army. If he finds them, this war will start to look a whole lot different."

"How do you know so much?"

"Young Hughes keeps me pretty well informed, Mary. He's sharp, and his newspaper gets all the reports, even though his editor will only print those that show the Confederacy in a favorable light."

In midsummer 1862, Mary began to suspect that something besides the war was going to require her attention. Soon, she was certain enough that she informed Cal that another child was on the way.

Cal was surprised. "Wow, I wasn't expecting that. It's been almost seven years since your pregnancy with Ellen. When do you think this baby will be born?"

"Sometime in February if my calculations are correct."

"At least I won't be fifty yet."

"Lots of men father babies after they're fifty, Cal."

"Fathering a baby is one thing; living to raise it is a different matter."

"I intend to keep you around a long, long time, Cal Nance."

"Let's hope so, Mary. I don't want to leave you saddled with a child to raise by yourself."

Due to the worries over the war, Mary's pregnancy was more stressful than her previous pregnancies but otherwise uneventful. A healthy baby boy was born on February 21, 1863, and named Franklin Taylor. Cal seemed pleased to have another son. Mary was just glad to have a healthy baby.

Chapter 15

War on the Doorstep

Even though the actual fighting had not come close to the farm, Cal and Mary followed the war's progress closely. They were well aware that all of Tennessee west of the Cumberlands was in federal hands late in 1862 and that a struggle for Chattanooga was a major focus of the war in the first part of 1863. Cal said he figured it was clear that Knoxville would be the next goal. The goal for Knoxville was delayed, however, by a strong attempt by the Confederates to retake middle Tennessee. Then the struggle for Chattanooga turned into a protracted battle that lasted for months. It was not until September that General Burnside and his federal troops seized Knoxville with virtually no resistance.

The newspaper where Marshall Hughes worked closed its doors immediately, and the editor and all employees fled, fearing arrest or worse. Marshall came to Cal and Mary seeking a safe haven. He and Sarah had announced their engagement in August and had even obtained a marriage license. Cal and Mary of course provided sanctuary but suggested that his presence remain a secret lest he, and perhaps their home, become a target for bushwhackers.

With Marshall no longer in Knoxville, it became hard for Cal and Mary to get news of exactly what was happening in the war. In early November, Mary's Uncle Samuel sent a message saying that he had been ordered by the federals to grind all wheat he had on hand. Also his hogs had all been taken except for four left for the family by order of the commanding officer. Eliza and daughters Lizzie and Annie had gone to stay with relatives at a site presumed to be safer than Shields Station.

Cal remarked to Mary that it was reassuring that the army was leaving some food behind for family use but he thought it prudent to hide part of their food supply nevertheless. They immediately began to plan what they could hide and where the best hiding places were. Cal said he figured that the items most in demand by the army would be the live animals, cured meat, flour and meal, dried beans, and potatoes.

"There isn't any way to hide our cattle, mutton, and hogs, but we can possibly find a place to hide some hams and other cured meat. For foods without much odor, like our beans, flour, and meal, we can hide some in the wall behind the closet. Hams and bacon are more challenging. The only place I can think where we might hide those items is that small cave on the cliff down the river. It's only accessible by boat and someone agile enough to climb the bank a little way. We'll have to leave enough of everything in the pantry and smokehouse to avoid suspicion. That's about all I can think of, Mary. What do you think?"

"I think we should also hide most of our coffee and sugar. Also our salt. Doesn't that make sense?"

"Yes, it does, and hiding those things won't require much space. I'll ask Hamilton and John to take care of the hams and bacon tomorrow. They can take an empty barrel to the cave and then put the meat in the barrel to keep animals out. They can pretend to be fishing on the river to keep from arousing the suspicion of anyone who sees them on the river in a skiff."

Because of the war, Marshall and Sarah had postponed their wedding but decided now that they wanted to wait no longer. Hamilton went to New Market for the minister, and the marriage took place on November 3. The minister said it might be some time before he could have the marriage recorded at the courthouse. Marshall Hughes breathed a sigh of relief, and Cal asked the minister to delay recording the marriage as long as possible. "Knowledge of this young man's presence here could put us all in danger. I am trusting you, as a man of God, to help keep us safe."

The minister didn't hesitate to indicate his willingness to comply. "Cal, you've known me a long time. I think you know I can be trusted. This marriage certificate will not be filed until you give me your approval. This war requires a bit of bending of ordinary procedures. Furthermore, no one is going to hear from my lips that this marriage has occurred."

A quiet supper with the family and a cake baked by Polly followed the exchange of vows. No other celebration was possible. When the cake was being served, Mary couldn't help but remember the elaborate party planned by her Aunt Eliza when she and Cal married. She squeezed Cal's hand and wondered if he was remembering the same thing. In spite of herself, tears came to her eyes. She didn't know if she was crying because the wedding of her eldest daughter couldn't have been as perfect as hers or the fact that she was no longer the young woman beginning life with a partner she adored.

Toward the end of the month, Doctor Sam sent word that he had heard that Confederate troops were on the outskirts of Knoxville and planning an attempt to retake the city. Only later would Cal and Mary learn of the disastrous attack by Longstreet's men on the main fort in Knoxville

A few days later, Sam sent a rider with an urgent message that there was fighting on his property. His message was terse. "Fighting almost on my doorstep! My home now a hospital! Thousands of rebel troops fleeing. Some headed your way; others toward Rutledge."

After the failed attack in Knoxville, General Longstreet and his troops had fled up the valley with the federal troops in hot pursuit. When the federal troops caught up with the Longstreet's army, a skirmish ensued at Blaine's Crossroads. The Confederate troops had already suffered heavy casualties at Knoxville, and Longstreet mostly wanted to escape with his remaining army.

Cal tried to be reassuring. "They're probably in too much of a hurry to bother with us, but we do need to be alert. I want Marshall and John to take turns being lookouts from the upstairs bedrooms. George, you run home and ask Hamilton to be ready to protect his boys, your mother, and Polly."

The watch didn't have to be in effect long. Within the hour, Marshall came to report that he could hear the sound of troops marching on the road leading to the ferry. "I can't see them because of the trees and how dark it is, but I definitely hear them."

All night the sound of the marching continued, and in the morning, the ferry could be seen crossing the river trip after trip, carrying as many men as possible each trip. In warmer weather, the men could have forded the river with the water level as low as it was, but the December weather wouldn't permit that even for the officers on horseback.

"Can you tell how many there are?" queried Mary.

"No, I have no idea," was Cal's reply. "They just keep coming and are amassed at the river's edge, waiting for the ferry. As soon as one bunch crosses, they head toward New Market while the ferry comes back across for the next load. I see a fire down by the river, perhaps for warmth or maybe for cooking. I wouldn't be surprised if we're not missing a pig or two, but that's the least of our worries."

By evening, the marching had ceased, and the ferry was no longer making trips back and forth. Except for remnants of several small fires and a few pork bones, all evidence of the rebel troops was gone.

The December weather turned bitter cold after that. Cal and Mary hoped that they had seen the last of troops in any color uniform. Indeed they did not see any more troops until December 20 when a few federal troops showed up with orders to obtain supplies for the army. They were polite, took what they wanted, and gave Cal a receipt. The officer in charge instructed Cal to hold onto the receipt so he could request recompense after the war's end.

Although most of their cattle, mutton, and hogs and a large quantity of potatoes, meal, flour, and beans were taken, Cal was relieved that their losses were not greater. "At least they didn't take everything. They asked how many there were in the family and how many people total on the farm were dependent on the food supply. We have enough food to get us through the winter, and they left breed stock of the animals. We will survive."

Christmas couldn't help but be bleak. There was no celebration of any sort. Mary was glad that baby Frank wasn't old enough to be disappointed by the lack of festivity, and Eliza, at age twelve, was fully aware of the circumstances surrounding this Christmas.

Shortly after Christmas, Mary's Uncle Samuel was able to send word that except for his patients and a few troops left as guards and caretakers, the rest of the federal troops had returned to Knoxville. After Cal had time to think about the ramifications of the news from

Sam, he shared a serious concern with the entire household.

"The Confederate troops appear to be long gone, and the federal troops are apparently wintering in Knoxville. Anybody we see in uniform now is likely to be a bushwhacker regardless of color of uniform. Marshall, John, and I are all carrying weapons, and I have also armed Hamilton and George. While a lot of people are opposed to arming slaves, in my view they're part of our family and have an equal right to protect themselves."

It was Mary's turn to speak. "Cal, is that the extent of your plan – that the men all carry weapons?"

"Well, Mary, we do have the hiding place. Probably Sarah, Eliza, and you could all fit in."

"You seem to be forgetting that we have an infant who is less than a year old. There is no way I'm getting in that space without him, and if I got in there with him, he might well cry and give away our hiding spot. From the reports we've heard in the past, even the bushwhackers don't usually murder women and children. I suggest that Marshall and you are the ones who need to hide. The bushwhackers would be willing to torture you or kill you to try to force you to disclose where you've hidden money."

"Mary, I'm afraid I'm known as someone who has made a bit of money. If I don't have any money anywhere for the bushwhackers to find, that would be highly suspicious."

"Fine, send Hamilton to Shields Station to see if Uncle Samuel might still have a cheap wallet for sale. Put some Confederate bills in it and leave it where it can be found. That money is almost worthless anyway, but maybe a bushwhacker would find that and leave."

"I hope you're right, but I still don't think it's right for me to hide and leave you exposed to possible harm."

"You said John is armed."

"True."

"Then, please quit arguing with me. I'm not getting in that hiding place. So you might as well. Oh, and please ask Hamilton to find out how Uncle Samuel is doing. We haven't heard from him since shortly after

Christmas. If he is still tending to injured troops, I want to make sure he is alright."

When Hamilton returned from Shields Station, he reported to Cal that the place was scarcely recognizable as the place they'd always known. Every room except for one and a part of the store was being used as a hospital. "Doctor Sam said to tell you that he is alright but pretty tired. The store is hardly operational now, mainly because he can't get supplies and because the Confederate money is so devalued by inflation that most people don't have enough funds to buy anything anyway."

"I guess all the folks being cared for are federal troops?"

"Most are, Mr. Cal, but I think from what Doctor Sam said there are a few rebels, too. He said something about having uniforms left at the door and everybody looking alike naked. I don't think the federals could argue with him much since he's the doctor."

"Yes, I can see where that would definitely give him some power despite the unusual circumstances."

"Oh, I forgot to tell you that he said he'd heard that Longstreet's group has apparently hunkered down for the winter at Russellville. Pity the poor folks there."

"Yes, they're probably being eaten out of house and home, and I bet Longstreet took over the nicest house in town for his winter quarters."

The dreary and bitter cold days of January slowly passed. In their isolation, the family knew nothing of what was happening with the war. They didn't even know that the long siege at Chattanooga had finally ended just before Christmas with a federal victory. They would scarcely have even been able to keep up with the days except for an old calendar from the previous year they used by advancing the days.

It was an unusually warm day in early February when John and George came running in from outside to say they had seen two men in uniform fording the river on horseback.

Mary immediately took control. "George, you go home in case you're needed there. Cal and Marshall, get upstairs and into the hiding place. Please hurry."

It seemed to Mary that she had barely gotten the words out of her mouth when there was a loud knock on the front door. Seeking a way to give the men more time to get to their hiding place, Mary gave unusual instructions to Eliza who happened to be holding the baby. "Eliza, pinch the baby, hard!"

As little Frank started to wail, Mary grabbed him from Eliza and headed toward the front door. On the way, she pinched him again as she called out loudly, "I'm coming; just a minute."

Heart pounding, Mary opened the front door, praying all the time that Cal and Marshall had made it to the safety of the wall behind the closet. Somehow, she managed to stay calm as she acted like she was consoling her infant.

"Please excuse the wailing. My baby is just learning to walk and fell and hurt himself. What can I do for you gentlemen?"

"We're here to search your house, ma'am – see if you're hiding any rebels. We know they were through here not long ago and thought you might have taken in a stray."

Mary didn't think the men were actually federal troops although their bedraggled uniforms were clearly dark blue. A dark stain on one uniform looked suspiciously like blood. "Probably took that uniform off a dead or injured soldier," Mary thought to herself.

"Why certainly. You're more than welcome to look around. My son John will be happy to show you around. He's just down the hall talking to his brother who is an invalid."

"Any other men folk here? Where's your husband?"

"We have a very large farm. I have no idea where my husband might be. He said something this morning about it being such a nice day that he might check fence lines to see if any need repair. The room to your right is the parlor, and the room to your left is the library. Beyond that is the bedroom where my other son stays now so he doesn't have to climb the stairs. He has a heart problem. The last room down here is the dining room. Upstairs are four bedrooms. You're more than welcome to search the entire house."

Mary started to call John but realized he was already standing near her in the entry hall. By this time, baby Frank's wailing had subsided to a muffled snubbing sound as Mary continued to pat his back as she cradled him against her shoulder.

"John, please show these gentlemen around. They say they need to search our house for Confederates."

Mary prayed that John would be civil. These men were clearly armed. For that matter, so was John, but there were two of them.

John began the tour of the house, one hand on the pistol in the pocket of his jacket. Mary listened to the sounds of the men going through the rooms and floor boards creaking upstairs. After what seemed like an eternity, she heard them coming down the stairs again, and she heard one asking John about the kitchen.

"We didn't see a kitchen. Where's your kitchen? We know you have to have one."

"John, will you please show these gentlemen the kitchen?"

As they headed out the back door, Mary prayed for Polly's safety. She didn't know that George had warned Polly as he headed home, and Polly had gone to her cabin and bolted the door.

When the men finally rode away, Mary sent John to tell his father and Marshall that they could emerge from hiding. The entire family gathered in Shields' room, and John shared the details of the tour of the house.

"Those two looked behind every curtain and under every bed. They pounded on every bed, too. I guess to see if anybody was hiding in the straw ticks or featherbeds. They looked in every dresser drawer, and I had to bite my tongue to keep from asking what size Confederate they thought might be hiding in a dresser drawer. When they got to your bedroom, Dad, one of them took the wallet you had left out. I pretended I didn't see that. Of course they looked in the closet, too. You may have heard them sliding clothes hangers around. Then they wanted to go up to the attic, and I took them up there. They opened the trunks, pawed around, and then sat down on the big trunk on top of the trap door and sat there complaining because they hadn't found anything except the wallet of Confederate money."

"What were you doing while they sat there talking?"

"I just stood there hoping they wouldn't decide to move the trunk. One of the men said he thought sure they would have found some silver or gold or expensive jewelry in a house like this. Then the other man complained about being hungry, and they decided to go look for food. When they got to the kitchen, Polly wasn't there. They found some leftover cornbread and beans, ate that, and one crammed a cold biscuit into his pocket. I think the other one took some coffee from the pantry. Then they left, headed toward the river."

"John, I was so afraid to send you to guide the men on the tour of the house, but I didn't know what else to do. You were very brave and very mature. I'm proud of you, son."

"I would have shot one of them if I needed to, Mother. I had my hand on my pistol almost the entire time."

Thankfully, there were no more instances of bushwhackers, but the family remained on edge the rest of the winter. When spring came and farmers began to be out in their fields and moving about in the community, all information gleaned from Cal's brothers and cousins across the river in Jefferson County seemed to indicate that the chance of bushwhackers now seemed remote. A few federal troops were guarding the rail line through nearby New Market, and there were federal troops still posted at Shields Station. Bushwhackers likely knew that federal troops would not take kindly to men pretending to be soldiers.

Mail delivery, which had been non-existent over the winter, resumed in the spring, and Mary received a letter from her sister saying that both her sons were prisoners of war. Samuel had been captured in Knoxville and was being held at Camp Douglas. William was captured at Lancaster, Kentucky, and was being held at Fort Camp Chase, Delaware. Mary read the letter to Cal and voiced her relief that her nephews were alive. "At least they're alive and apparently uninjured. We can pray for this war to end before more lives are sacrificed."

With the immediate countryside seemingly safe now, trips to both New Market and Shields Station resumed, and the family was able to keep abreast of war news. Knoxville newspapers were delivered by train to New Market, and Mary's Uncle Samuel had access to war news from the troops stationed at the hospital.

It was clear now that the Confederacy was in shambles. Grant's success at Chattanooga had finally broken the Nashville to Atlanta supply line. With that supply line fractured and the Mississippi River firmly in federal control, the Confederacy had few means with which to re-equip its battered army. Meanwhile, supplies and federal reinforcements poured in from the north. Moreover, the longer the war lasted, the more difficult it became for the Confederacy to fund its struggle. With money running low for financing the war, the southern states just printed more money, adding to the problem of inflation.

While it seemed evident that more battles in east Tennessee were unlikely, the war continued to take a heavy toll on supplies of all kinds. It was almost impossible to purchase coffee, and sugar was nonexistent. Mary was grateful for what they had hidden months before but knew that supply wouldn't last long. They could use molasses and honey to sweeten items needing such, but coffee would soon be a thing of the past unless they could make a substitute concoction of some sort. Thanks to the hams and bacon they had stored in the cave, they had plenty of meat. The beans and potatoes they had hidden would see them through the coming months and provide for the spring planting.

Cal noted to Mary that one of the big differences for the farm this spring would be fewer animals. The army had taken twenty hogs and twenty sheep in addition to the wheat, potatoes, salt pork, and lard they had appropriated. The latter items could more easily be replaced than the animals; it would take time to amass that many hogs and sheep again. The loss of those hogs and sheep would mean virtually none to sell this year, not that many people had money to spend anyway.

Grateful that the active fighting had moved to other arenas, Cal and all of the other men on the farm set about planting the wheat, corn, and field crops. Mary, who was still nursing one year old Frank, was not very free to help with planting the large garden, but all of the other women and Hamilton's two boys worked on that endeavor. As the planting began, Mary expressed her gratitude and hopes to Polly and Lucy.

"They took the majority of our animals, but they didn't take our seeds and soil. Cal started this farm with very little before we married. Now, to some extent, we're starting over."

Cal and Mary continued to follow news of the war closely, hoping the war would end soon, but the Confederates continued to fight even though its army was in shreds and its supplies limited. "All we can do," Cal told Mary, "is live the best we can each day. I think this farm will be profitable again, but it's going to take a long time for the economy of this entire region to recover."

"Do you think the army will come for our food and animals again this fall?"

"It's possible, Mary, but I doubt it. From what I've surmised, most of the troops that were in the Knoxville area last fall have been moved to other theaters of the war. That means much less food will be needed to feed the troops left there. We'll take pains again to hide enough provisions to get all of us here through the next year, but beyond that, there's not much we can do."

"What about the animals?"

"We can hide hams, shoulders, and other salt pork if we need, but there's no way to hide the live animals. If worst comes to worst, we can live off of chickens, squirrels, rabbits, and fish from the river. The army is not going to take those."

"How many of our animals gave birth this spring?"

"Four sows each had large litters, ranging from nine to eleven piglets. Five ewes gave birth, but those were all single births. As you can see, it will take a long time to build up our mutton stock again. Three of the lambs are female, so that is good. Also, six cows have had calves, so we'll have plenty of milk and butter for the next year."

Much to Mary's relief, the large garden did well and provided ample amounts of everything from spring lettuce and green onions to beans, peas, tomatoes, beets, okra, peppers, cabbage, cucumbers, and potatoes. All of the women stayed busy all summer breaking beans, shelling peas, making kraut, and pickling beets and cucumbers. Greens were planted for fall harvesting, and apples were dried when the apple trees produced in the early fall. When the cane was ready, Cal and Hamilton made molasses.

In the fall, they heard of Atlanta's fall to union forces in September followed by Sherman's march to the sea and his scorched earth policy. "Surely, this terrible war will end soon," Mary told Cal.

"I don't see any other possibility, Mary, but I fear the south is going to pay a huge price for years to come, a price in the thousands upon thousands of lives lost and an economy in ruins."

"I guess I'm trying to focus on our blessings, Cal. We've lost a lot in recent years, including two of our precious children, but we still have each other and five of our children including little Frank. Maybe God sent him to us to help us get over our other losses. The army took part of our animals and other food supplies last fall, but they didn't take our spirit."

"You amaze me, Mary Graham. After all these years, you still amaze me."

"You haven't called me Mary Graham in over twenty years. That sounded strange."

"Still glad you married me and changed your name?"

"Every day, Cal, every day."

Chapter 16

After the War

As soon as Cal heard the news about the new Tennessee constitution which abolished slavery in February, 1865, he called all nine adult slaves on his property to assemble in the dining room of his home. The legislature had wisely chosen to not wait until the end on the war to act on this important matter, and Cal didn't want to wait any longer either. As soon as the group assembled, Cal began to speak.

"One of you asked to come here. Another of you I purchased because I thought it was the only way to protect you, and the rest of you became my responsibility upon the death of my father over twelve years ago. I think most of you know that ever since 1833, the manumission law in the state of Tennessee required that any slave given freedom had to leave the state within one year. Whether my thinking was right or wrong, I didn't think that was a good option for any of you. I didn't know where you would go or what you could do. From 1854 on, manumission was completely illegal in this state. Yes, there were a few free Negroes in Tennessee, but they were either freed prior to 1833 or were born to free people of color."

The little group waited expectantly as Cal continued his explanation of the recent change in the law and its implication. "As you know, this country has been embroiled in a costly and deadly war for the last four years over the issue of slavery. That war has to come to an end soon, and I think even the most ardent supporters of the Confederacy see the inevitability of that. Our legislators in Nashville certainly do, and on February 22, they approved a new state constitution which abolishes slavery. I've called you together to tell you that you are free! You can choose to leave or choose to stay. If you choose to stay, I'll pay you what I can. The animals, wheat, and other things taken by the army in December last year left me with virtually no income for the year, and I don't know if this year will be much better. The Confederate money we're still using is worthless, and the U.S. dollars used to purchase those deeds of promise are gone. I tell you all of that to let you know exactly what my situation is."

"If you choose to stay, you will have the guarantee of a warm cabin, food for nourishment, and medical care when you need it. We'll work together as we always have, and I will pay you a salary best as I can. Now, if you choose to leave, you go with my blessing, but please, please let me know that you're leaving so that Mary and I will not be worried that something has happened to you."

Polly was the first to speak. "I'm not going anywhere, Mr. Cal. I asked to come here, and you were kind enough to accommodate my request. I love this family and this place. Besides, I'm too old to be striking out on my own."

Lucy spoke up next. "You rescued me and my twin babies from a terrible situation. Miss Mary nursed my George at her own breast, and George and John are like brothers. If Hamilton leaves, he'll leave without me. George can make up his own mind when he's older. He's just fourteen."

One by one, the rest of the group spoke, including Hamilton, who said there wasn't any way he'd leave without Lucy. Only Dick, the one young man without a wife or consort, indicated that he would like to leave. In response to Dick's stated intention of leaving, Cal asked him to please come by the house before he actually left.

Cal later told Mary that he planned to retrieve a bit of silver for Dick and provide him with a letter of reference. When Cal gave the money and the letter to Dick, he also gave him a horse, not the best horse on the property but one that was still serviceable, as well as directions to the businesses owned by Mary's uncles in Morristown.

After Dick's departure, Cal started trying to figure out what he could pay the remaining workers and whether he was going to have any money to pay them before the sale of pigs and wheat later in the year. Although the war wasn't quite over, its coming end was readily apparent.

In the waning days of the war, a welcome distraction from the war news was the pending birth of

Cal and Mary's first grandchild. Daughter Sarah was expecting a baby most any day, and on March 9, baby Mary Ellen Hughes was born in the same home where her grandparents had lived since their marriage in 1842. After the birth, Mary said to Cal, "Can you believe we're grandparents? I don't feel like a grandmother; I have a two year old child."

Cal's reply was reassuring as was his custom. "Well, you're one fine looking granny, and you are only forty."

"Still, how the years have passed. In May, we will have been married twenty-three years, and I'll be forty-one."

"Just remember, Mary, every time you mention your age, I have to add eleven more for my age."

Spring planting was well underway when the news came of Lee's surrender at Appomattox, Virginia. General Joseph Johnson surrendered the rest of the Army of The Tennessee a few days later. The war was finally over. Most of east Tennessee had perhaps fared better than the rest of the state, but massive problems remained. The economy was in shambles as Cal had predicted, and most families had lost one or more members in the bloody battles that had been fought. Cal and Mary could only be grateful that they had the means to start over and the loyalty of most of their former slaves.

Cal assured Mary that although their cash on hand was limited to the silver and gold coins he'd buried during the early part of the war, he had other investments that should be profitable in the future. He had bonds from Jefferson, Anderson, and Washington County purchased before the war, and stock in the East Tennessee, Virginia, and Georgia Railroad. There were also several small loans he'd made to individuals, but he was doubtful that most of them would ever be repaid because the war had left those individuals destitute.

Cal also explained his plans for retrieving the buried coins. "I'm not going to dig up all the buried coins at one time. There's still too much danger of thievery. First I'm going to dig up that portion buried under the manure. I'm tired of changing out the patty to keep it looking fresh. Those coins will provide cash to purchase essentials we may need and money I can use to begin paying these loyal individuals who have chosen to stay here. When I'm sure that banks are secure, I'll open an account in one with part of the rest of the money. Perhaps I'll invest some in county bonds. Those don't usually mature for thirty years. I might live to see their maturity, but if not, that investment will be there for my heirs. My biggest immediate concern is whether the weather will be favorable for our crops this year and whether there'll be anyone with enough money to purchase the wheat, corn, and hogs. I don't plan to sell any mutton this year. I need to build up their numbers first."

Mary's relief at hearing Cal's listing of their assets was almost palpable. "Oh, Cal, that is a relief. I assumed we were in much worse circumstances than what you've described."

"We are a lot better off than many people, Mary, but we still have to be very careful with our finances. Those county bonds I mentioned aren't due to mature until 1876 and 1878. We would soon be without any cash if we pay our loyal household and farm helpers solely from the cash on hand. We desperately need for the farm to be profitable again. I don't even know yet what I can afford to pay everyone and what amount is fair. I must give them something soon as a commitment of my faithfulness to the promise I made them. I'm thinking of trying to pay each one a base amount each month and an additional amount based on the farm profits."

With those plans in place, life on the farm settled into a new normal. The people living on the farm were the same people, but relationships had changed. Every former slave living there was now there by choice, not by ownership papers and laws.

Soon after the war ended, Marshall Hughes talked with Cal about what he should plan to do.

"I feel like I've taken advantage of your hospitality for the last year and a half. Now that the war is over, I could probably find work in Knoxville again, but I hear that the situation there is quite dire. Thousands of new people flooded into town during the war years, and there is almost no housing available. Cases of retribution for Civil War actions are a common occurrence, even to the point of pistol duels on the sidewalk. Also, reports in the Knoxville paper indicate that city streets are filthy and disease is rampant. Just last fall there was a smallpox epidemic. While I want to get back to work and support my wife and child, I don't want to bring disease into this household."

"I appreciate that, Marshall, but I think the best way for you to support your wife and child right now is to stay right here. I know that farming is not your chosen line of work, but there might be some other opportunities available. One of the stores in New Market might need a clerk, or you could seek a position in Morristown with one of Mary's uncles or her brother-in-law. I don't know what might be available right now. I do know that Milton's paper mill burned down during the war. If you took a position in New Market, you could just ride over there every day. A position in Morristown is not compatible with traveling back and forth every day. However, you could board there during the week and take the train back to New Market on the weekends. We could take a horse over to meet you. The other option is to stay right here and pretend to be a farmer until the world settles down a bit."

It turned out there were no available positions at either New Market or Morristown related to Marshall's experience, so he decided to take Cal up on the offer of "pretending to be a farmer" for a while. Although not his chosen line of work, the respite from operating printing presses gave him time to think about changes that could make printing easier. When he wasn't checking fences or helping newborn lambs stay warm, he began to make diagrams and a description of a revolutionary process he could patent.

While Cal focused on the farm, Mary focused on the joys and challenges of parenting a lively two year old while providing assistance to new mother Sarah and caring for son Shields in his still fragile state. It seemed at times to Mary that she was pulled in several different directions, but she had no other choice. Life had dealt her a complicated set of circumstances. She was doing the best she could to deal with them.

Summer passed. The farm was reasonably productive, but selling farm produce was more of a challenge, precisely for the reason Cal had predicted. Few people had money to buy anything, regardless of need. Cal was able to sell some corn and wheat to a couple of local millers who planned to grind and bag meal and flour for sale directly to customers who had not been able to put in crops themselves.

Mary's Uncle Samuel purchased some of the meal and flour for sale in his store. The last of the injured soldiers were gone, but efforts to get Shields Station back to full operation were at a standstill. Stage coach service had ceased during the war so there was no hope of the inn being profitable again. Uncle Samuel told Cal and Mary that he was glad he had his medical practice and the store for income.

As 1865 came to a close, Cal shared his hopes with Mary. "This year hasn't been too bad, all things considered. Maybe next year will be better."

The year 1866 was profitable enough for the farm that Cal was able to purchase four small Hawkins County bonds. The overall economy wasn't much better than at the end of the war, but at least the farm seemed to be headed toward stability. Cal was less optimistic about the state and national scene with radical Parson Brownlow serving as Tennessee governor and Andrew Johnson as a president ill equipped to restore order to a fractured nation. He could only hope that another election would restore some modicum of sanity to those offices. Meanwhile, he had his own little part of the universe to tend. That was all he could reasonably worry about.

As Christmas 1866 approached, Mary suggested to Cal that they try to pay some attention to the holiday. "Cal, last year at Christmas we were just getting our heads above water, so to speak. Surely this year we can really celebrate Christmas. Frank is almost four, and our little granddaughter is nearly two. They would both enjoy a few gifts, nothing elaborate, but something to acknowledge the season. It might cheer Eliza a bit also. I think she's still despondent at times over the loss of her little sisters."

"Mary, I agree that doing something to celebrate Christmas this year is a good idea, but are you sure that it isn't you who is still despondent?"

"Of course I am. It's something that will always be a part of me, but I'm trying to focus on what I have. We've talked about this before."

"That's true. I shouldn't even have brought that up. Why don't you think about what you want to do for the children? Also, let's do something extra for Polly, Lucy, and all the other employees and their children. I think we can afford to do that."

Christmas was celebrated as planned. Cal, John, and George cut down a good sized cedar tree from the pasture and set it up in the parlor. Mary, Sarah, Eliza, and Lucy decorated it, making sure there was nothing harmful in reach of little Mary Ellen. Mary thought it good to have a reason to have cheer in the house again, and it was a special joy to see the children open their gifts. Lucy and Polly prepared a delicious meal, and the entire day was special. To make the day extra special and as a reminder of why Christmas is celebrated, Cal and Hamilton had set up a manger scene in the barn, minus a baby of course, and Cal took Frank and all of the younger children on the farm to see it, explaining that baby Jesus had slept in a bed like that.

It was less than a month after that joyous Christmas that tragedy struck the family again. Son Shields developed what at first seemed to be only a cold. Then came bronchitis, then a fever, and finally difficulty breathing. Mary's Uncle Samuel was sent for and came promptly. He listened to Shields' chest and then spoke to Cal and Mary in another room. With tears in his eyes, Doctor Sam explained the situation.

"The boy has pneumonia, and I am fearful that his heart is not going to be able to stand the strain. You know how much I've always loved this boy. Not only is he your oldest son, he was named for me. I wish there were something I could do for him, but I can't offer much. We can try some mustard plasters on his chest and a little whiskey and peppermint for his cough, but that's about it I'm afraid."

Samuel Shields Nance died on January 29, 1867, age twenty years, six months, and twenty-five days. On a cold and barren January 31, the family made their way across the river on the ferry and up the hill to the little cemetery. As Mary stood trembling at the graveside, the same thought kept playing in her head. "Three of my children, three of my precious children now lie on this hill. Lord, please, please let my four remaining children outlive me!" She was barely aware of Cal's comforting arm about her waist.

Later, Mary told Cal, "I guess I always knew this day was coming. From the time that Shields didn't recover from the fever that sickened him and Eliza, this day was inevitable. Like you once told me, to be alive means we have to suffer from time to time. The last few days have been another one of those times. Now I have a four year old...well four in a few days, who doesn't understand why his mama is sad. You know what that means, Cal?"

"Yes, it means you're going to wash your face, go hug that four year old, and tell him that his brother is sick no more. Then you'll ask Sarah to bake a cake for Frank while you play with Mary Ellen."

Somehow, it didn't seem to Mary as difficult to get over her grief this time. Maybe it was because she had little Frank to focus on, but she thought it more likely that it was because so much of her grieving had been done in advance.

Mary decided to focus on her role as mother to Frank and grandmother to little Mary Ellen for at least the next few months. In the fall, she would take on her role as teacher again, teacher for Frank and for the children of the farm's employees. Mary thought to herself how nice it was to be able to think of these folks as employees now, not slaves. She hoped their lives were enough changed that they felt different too. She knew that Cal had talked with all of them about saving a portion of their earnings toward their children's education or toward the purchase of property.

It was toward the end of that year that Sarah told her mother that she was to be grandmother for the second time. Another baby should arrive mid-summer. Now, that was something to look forward to for sure.

It was also toward the end of the year that the family received quite a surprise. They were eating supper one evening when they heard a knock on the back door. Cal said, "I'll get it," and headed toward the door. As he opened the door, everyone at the table heard him say, "My word! I can't believe my eyes. Come in, come in. We're just having a bite to eat. You're just in time to join us."

There stood a very disheveled and weary looking Dick, the former slave who had decided to strike out on his own as soon as he was freed. "Are you sure, Mr. Cal? I know I look a mess."

"So, you can clean up later. Right now, I bet you can use some food."

"Yes, sir, I am pretty hungry, but first I want to get straight to the point. Is there any way you can see fit to let me come back here to stay? I didn't know how hard life could be until I left here."

"You can tell us where you've been and what has happened to you after you eat. Then we'll talk about what your pay will be for your work here."

Chapter 17

Autumn Years

As a new decade began, Mary thought of everything the previous decade had brought: the illness of Shields and Eliza, the start of a war, the death of Ellen Joannah, the courtship and marriage of her oldest daughter, the birth of Frank, the army taking most of their crops and animals in December 1863, Cal and Marshall Hughes hiding in the wall behind the closet, the freeing of slaves, birth of a grandchild, economic challenges, the death of Shields, and the birth of a second grandchild, Lucy Ann, on July 11, 1868. Also near the end of the decade, Polly had decided to go live with Sibby.

Mary could only hope that the new decade would be less tumultuous, but wondered if that was even remotely possible. The sheer number of relatives getting on in years made it almost inevitable that there would be deaths in the family in the next few years.

The first few years of the decade went smoothly. Productivity of the farm increased. Sarah's husband found work in New York City and sent for Sarah and the girls to join him. Mary continued to teach young Frank and other youngsters on the farm, and John and Eliza matured into young adults.

Almost three years of the 1870s decade passed before there were any major changes in the family. Then ten days before Christmas of 1872, Cal's mother died. She was eighty-six years old and had outlived Cal's dad by twenty years. Mary hoped that her mother-in-law had been happy in her second marriage but still thought it sad that Cal's dad had preceded his wife in death by that many years. She remembered that her mother-in-law had given her reason for remarrying as hating to be alone. "How terrible to be a widow for so long," Mary thought to herself. "I don't think I could bear to be without Cal for that long."

After the burial, the family gathered at Cal and Mary's home because of its proximity to the family cemetery. There was quite a bit of laughter associated with family stories, especially the anecdotes describing discipline meted out by the deceased.

When all the relatives had left, Cal sat at the dining table and stared out the window toward the hill across the river, the hill containing the fresh grave of his mother. "You know," he said to Mary, "as long as you have one of your parents still living, it seems like a barrier between you and the grave. When that last parent dies, you realize you're next in line. That barrier is gone."

"I guess I never thought of it like that, Cal. I was only eight when my mother died, scarcely aware of the finality of death and certainly not focused on my own mortality. For all practical purposes, I lost my father at the same time. Yes, I loved him, and I cried when he died in that horrible fire, but I truly lost him when I was eight. I hear what you're saying, but guess I never felt that sense of a barrier between myself and the grave."

Christmas was celebrated that year but seemed somewhat muted. There were no little children in the house with Sarah and the children in New York. Mary hoped that Sarah would bring the children home for the summer, but knew it would be a hard trip on the train. Perhaps she shouldn't get her hopes up. Still, she couldn't help but hope. She knew Sarah didn't like New York and disliked it even more in the summer.

When Christmas was over and the tree taken down, the winter days seemed cold and dreary. There was something depressing about the days getting dark so early. Mary liked to read but found that difficult to do by lamplight. She was pretty sure too that her eyesight wasn't what it once was. "I guess that's to be expected though," she said to herself. "I am going to be forty-nine on my birthday this year. I'm not going to mention my age to Cal, though. He always reminds me that he has to add eleven more years. I'm sure he'll say sixty is old."

The dim winter light also made it difficult for Mary to do sewing or mending at night, but she had discovered she could either crochet or knit almost without seeing what she was doing. Thus, she often passed the long evenings making sweaters, mittens, and caps for her granddaughters in New York. Sarah had written that it was very cold there.

As the days started to get longer in February and the first brave bulbs of spring began to emerge, Mary was almost jubilant. "I don't know when I've been so glad to see the first signs of spring," she told Cal.

"Ah, yes, that time of year when we plow and plant and plow and plant and pray there won't be a late freeze. That time of year when I may be bringing a newborn lamb into the house to keep it warm or out in the field looking for a cow that is calving. Yes, the joys of spring."

"Cal, I've never heard you sound like that before. What's wrong?"

"I don't know, Mary. Maybe I'm just tired."

"If you're tired, give more of the work to John. He knows the farm, and he's mature enough to supervise. Just turn loose of a few things."

Later, Mary mused about the day's conversation, and she remembered what Cal had said right after his mother's death. "Maybe it's the barrier thing; maybe Cal is focused on his mortality and the idea that he's next in line for the grave. I don't know anything to say to make him feel better. I wish I did."

Spring did come, of course, and with it, Cal's mood seemed to lift. Mary hoped the positive change would last.

Also in the spring, Mary became aware that son John had a new interest. Every Sunday afternoon there wasn't a hard rain, John saddled up his horse and headed out for the afternoon. About dark, he would come home, tend to his horse, and come into the house, looking for leftover food. Finally, Mary's curiosity got the best of her.

"John, is it too much to ask that you let us know where you keep going on Sunday afternoon?"

"Oh, sure, I've just been riding up to Tampico."

"What's at Tampico?"

"A girl."

"Is that all you're going to tell me?"

"Well, I can tell you that I think she's a special girl. She's just a little younger than me. She was born in 1850 at Bluff City. Later, her father moved the family to Bristol for better school opportunities. In fact, he and his wife helped found a school for girls in Bristol. After the war, he was Mayor of Bristol for a term or two. Then they moved to Tampico, for financial reasons I think. Is that enough?"

"You've told me all about the father. What about the young lady? You didn't even mention her name."

"Oh, guess I didn't. Her name is Harriet Crumley, but she goes by Hattie. She's well educated and teaches school in a subscription school at Tampico. I don't know how many parents are paying to send their children there, but I do know she teaches all eight grades."

"She must have her hands full."

"You would be even more impressed if you could see how tiny she is. I'm sure she must have several pupils taller than she is, but she's a little spitfire. I imagine they don't give her much trouble."

"So when do we get to meet this young lady?"

"I guess you get to meet her when her daddy says you can meet her."

"Well, if you're as serious about her as it sounds like you are, I hope that will be soon."

John's courtship of Hattie continued over the summer, and in September he told his parents that he wanted to propose to Hattie as soon as he could figure out where they might live.

"Dad, I feel like you need me here on the farm, but I'm not going to ask you and Mother to let us live here. I remember when Sarah and Marshall lived here, I thought that was kind of awkward."

"Son, there's the house on the Perrin property that I bought some time back The house has been empty for a while now, but I think it's structurally sound. You could clean it up, do whatever repairs are needed and live there if you'd like."

"How much would the rent be?"

"You wouldn't need to pay rent. I figure if you're helping me run the farm, you deserve that much. Plus, I need to start paying you a salary or a percentage of the farm profits."

"I really appreciate that, Dad. I hadn't thought about that house, and I really like the idea of having a steady income."

"Obviously the house needs some paint but not a lot more. It may even have some broken windows, but those are an easy fix. When we get the major part of the harvest done, you'll have time to get busy on fixing the place up."

John and Hattie were married on November 6, 1873, at her parents' home in Tampico. Within a year, the young couple had provided Cal and Mary with another grandchild, Mignonette (Minnie) McBee Nance. Two years later their first son was born and named Ralph Ramsey. By late 1878, John and Hattie were expecting their third child, but that pending birth was the furthest thing from Mary's mind.

Shortly after Christmas, Cal remarked to Mary that he wasn't feeling well. When pressed for more information, he couldn't seem to be specific. "I don't know; I just don't feel good, and sometimes my heart feels like it does funny things."

"Like what?"

"I don't know. Maybe just beats real fast for a while."

"Why don't you get Uncle Samuel to take a look at you?"

"I don't mean to be disrespectful, Mary, but he's getting up in years. What is he, eighty?"

"No, I don't think he's quite that old yet."

"Well, he can't be far from it."

"If you don't trust Uncle Samuel anymore, see Dr. Taylor in New Market. He's a recent graduate of Vanderbilt Medical School in Nashville. He ought to be up on things."

The first nice day in January, Cal did pay Dr. Taylor a visit. When he came home, he told Mary that yes, the doctor had said his heart was "a little out of whack."

"I don't believe that is exactly what Dr. Taylor said, Cal."

"Well, he said something about my heart not beating right; said no medication had been shown to be helpful for the problem. He told me to take it easy and to lie down and be quiet for a while when my heart feels fluttery."

"Are you going to mind him? Are you going to take it easy?"

"Yes, I am. I stopped at John's house on the way home and told him he's in charge of all spring plowing and planting."

"I'm glad you're willing to listen to the doctor."

"The problem is I don't like feeling useless."

"You are not useless, Cal, and maybe you've just been pushing yourself too hard."

As weeks went by, Mary could tell that Cal was not feeling better. She noticed new symptoms such as him appearing to be out of breath after climbing the stairs. Knowing that Cal probably wouldn't admit that he needed to limit his activities any further, Mary pretended that it was she who needed to make a change in where they slept.

"Cal, it's so cold upstairs at night. Could we use the downstairs bedroom until spring?"

Cal agreed, and Mary quietly moved all of his clothing from the closet and dresser upstairs to a wardrobe and chest-of-drawers in the downstairs bedroom. Mary hoped the change would make a difference in Cal's health, but she saw no sign of improvement.

Mary was acutely aware that Cal was almost the exact same age his father had been when he died suddenly in 1852. She feared going to sleep at night lest she wake up with Cal beside her, stone-cold. Each night, she said the same prayer, "Please God, let Cal still be alive in the morning."

The third week of April, Cal told Mary that he thought perhaps Dr. Taylor should be asked to make a house call. Mary didn't hesitate; she immediately sent George to fetch the doctor. When Dr. Taylor arrived, he asked Mary to step out of the room while he examined Cal.

Mary waited in the dining room for what seemed like an eternity. When Dr. Taylor joined her, he was blunt.

"I hate to tell you this, Mrs. Nance, but I believe that your husband's heart is failing. His heart sounds much worse than when I saw him three months ago, and he has had some other symptoms which I believe he has hidden from you. Frankly, I don't expect him to live much longer."

"Does he know?"

"Oh, yes, he knows. In fact, he told me."

"Thank you, Dr. Taylor. I appreciate your honesty. How much do I owe you for today's visit?"

"There's no charge for the visit today, ma'am. This visit gave me a chance to get out in the fresh air for a while, but if you don't mind, I'll be on my way now. I did leave some pain pills at the bedside, and your husband paid me for them. Directions are with the medication."

Mary saw Dr. Taylor out the door and went immediately to the bedroom. Before she could open her mouth to say a word, Cal spoke.

"Mary, please don't try to say anything. We both know what is happening. Just find Frank. Tell him to take George with him and go bring Isaac Mitchell, Cousin Paschal, and your Uncle Samuel here. Together!"

Mary wanted to fling her arms around Cal and plead, "Please don't leave me," but she left the room to do his bidding.

After sending the boys on their way, Mary reentered the bedroom, determined not to break down and cry. She took Cal's hand, laid her head down on it and sat in silence for several minutes. Finally, when she felt she could speak without crying, she asked, "Why did you want Uncle Samuel to come? Did you want a second opinion?"

"No, I didn't want a second opinion. I just wanted him to be able to testify that I am of sound mind."

"Can I get you something to eat?"

"No, I don't feel like eating anything right now. Maybe later."

It was a little after 4:00 p.m. on April 25 when the three men gathered at Cal's bedside, and he started to dictate his last will and testament. By 6:00 p.m., he was finished.

The lengthy will specified the amount of cash Mary was to receive from the estate as well as all household furnishings, all coffee, sugar, and bacon on hand, and the exact number of farm animals that were to be her portion. The land itself was to be divided between the two sons with the north end of the property going to John and the south end, including the home residence, to son Frank. Although the south end was to be Frank's property, the will specified that Mary would have the use and control of the land during her lifetime. The will further specified that the two daughters were to receive a sum of cash from the estate equivalent to the value of the land given to the sons, thereby assuring that all four children were treated equal. A final stipulation was that both sons were to pay rent on the land to their mother during her lifetime, assuring her of a source of income.

When the will was completed and dated, it was signed by the three witnesses and Cal.

Three days later, Cal took his last breath as Mary sat by his bedside and watched him slowly slip away. George and John went to New Market to let Mr. Minnis know to send someone for the body. While they were gone, Mary continued to sit by the bedside, holding Cal's hand as it slowly turned cold. She looked at his arms and thought how strong they once were, how they had held her, and how those hands had caressed her. All that would be left now were the memories of almost thirty-seven years together.

When Mary stood in the cemetery for Cal's service, it was the first time that she had stood there without Cal's supportive arm about her. This time, her two sons stood with her.

Chapter 18

Widow

After the service in the cemetery, Mary, her two sons, Eliza, and a number of friends and family crossed on the ferry together to the house for a meal the neighbors had prepared. Later, the gathering seemed but a blur to Mary. She did recall that there was not the kind of jocularity that had been so evident when Cal's mother died, and she remembered that someone had remarked that Cal had still been a handsome man and looked too young to die.

When the group had dispersed, Eliza cleaned up the dining room and kitchen and suggested that her mother might need to lie down and rest.

"No, I don't think I can rest. I'm not sure what to do with myself right now. Your daddy brought me to this house almost thirty-seven years ago as an eighteen year old bride, and we shared this home through good and bad. Now, all I feel is the emptiness of him not being here, and I remember how my daddy said our house lost its soul when my mother died. He dealt with that loss by never living in the house again. I don't have that option. I have a son who isn't grown and a farm to operate. I think I'll go find Frank and see if he'll walk with me out to the barn to see the newborn lambs."

After returning from her walk, Mary told Frank that she believed she wanted to stay outside a little while longer by herself. She sat down on a large stump where she had a good view of the river and watched the water flow, dark and moving swiftly from recent rains. "Just like my life," Mary thought. "There's no holding it back. The river is carrying everything with it, and I can't see what is coming next." Mary sat, mesmerized by the river, until Eliza came out to check on her.

"Mother, you need to eat some supper. I've heated up some leftovers. Please come have a meal with Frank and me. I know you're missing Dad. Frank and I are also. John said to tell you he left to go check on Hattie and the children."

After supper, Mary told Frank and Eliza goodnight and went upstairs to her bedroom. Exhausted, she laid down on her bed, still dressed in the clothes she had worn all day. In the dim evening light, she looked around the room. "Oh, what memories this room holds," was the last thought she had before falling asleep from exhaustion.

Like a mechanized toy, Mary walked through the next few days, just putting one foot in front of the other and doing only what she had to do. She had endured loss before, even the loss of three of her children, but nothing had ever made her feel as totally empty as she felt now. After her other losses, she had been able to fill the emptiness in her heart by focusing on the needs of her other children. That wasn't the case now. Sure, Eliza and Frank missed their father, but they were hardly small children in need of cuddling. Frank was sixteen, and Eliza almost twenty-eight. "Eliza twenty-eight! Now, that's a shock to the senses. I was barely twenty-seven when she was born, and she was my fourth child. She hasn't had any serious suiters, although she's attractive enough. Have I held her back, over protected her because of the health problems she had? I hope not."

Mary had been aware of the fact that Cal dictated a will three days before his death, but she hadn't thought anymore about it until her Uncle Samuel sent a letter saying that his son Alonzo, now an attorney in Morristown, would be happy to read the will and discuss its contents at the family's convenience. Alonzo had suggested that he would be happy to save the family a trip to Morristown by meeting with the family on a Saturday when he came home to Shields Station.

So arrangements were made for the reading of the will, and the family assembled on a Saturday afternoon in May to hear its contents. Alonzo said he would notify Sarah of her share of the inheritance. After the will was read, Alonzo asked if there were any questions.

Mary was the first to speak. "I have a couple of questions. The will doesn't specify the number of animals that John is to receive, but I assume that there are adequate numbers that at least half are going to John."

"I have no idea about that, Mary. John likely knows. If not, you'll have to count the animals. If you think John is not getting his fair share, there is nothing to prevent you from gifting him with additional animals."

"I have one additional question. What does that mean about my sons having to pay rent on the land they're inheriting? I never heard of anything like that in a will."

"I think Mr. Cal just wanted to make sure that you're provided for. Your sons are named as co-executors of the will, but in as much as Frank is a minor, the major responsibility, actually pretty much the sole responsibility for now, will fall to John. I presume that your husband assumed that the rent would come from some portion of the farm income. Since he didn't specify a percentage, that amount will be up to the executor to determine. Also, remember that the will specifies that you are to retain control and use of Frank's portion during your lifetime. I trust that you can come to an amicable agreement on the rent issue… Are there any other questions?"

Hearing no other questions, Alonzo bid them all farewell.

After Alonzo left, Mary turned to John with a proposition. "John, neither Frank nor I have experience in managing a farm. Would you consider it a fair exchange if you oversee the work on my section of the farm in lieu of some payment of rent? You don't have to give me an answer right now if you don't want to, but think it over and let me know."

"I don't think I need to think it over, Mother. That way, the profits on my section of the farm will be entirely mine, and I won't have to worry about the rent issue."

"Good, we agree, and please remember that I'm asking you only to oversee the work on my section, not do the work. I trust that you will insure that the survey is made and that Alonzo files all the papers at the Grainger County Courthouse and provides deeds for all of us. The will mentioned a little book where your daddy kept a record of investments and loans he had made. I believe I know where that book is located and will get it for you…Oh, and by the way, John, I almost forgot. I think you know that your daddy has been paying all the employees a base salary plus a bonus based on the productivity of the farm. To me, it makes sense to leave the employees together as a group with me contributing half of the money for salaries. We can discuss this further after you've had time to check your dad's records. I wouldn't suggest paying them any less than what they've been making, not that I think you would."

It was soon after the reading of the will that Eliza mentioned to her mother that her cousin John had invited her to accompany him to watch a horse race in Knoxville. At first, Mary asked, "Which cousin John? You do have more than one, you know."

"John Noah, Mother. He promises it will be a lot of fun. He suggested we ride over to New Market, leave our horses at the livery stable for the day, take the train to Knoxville to see the race, and then take the train back. The days are long now, so we should be back before dark."

"That sounds alright to me, Eliza. I wouldn't like to see you going off with just anybody on an excursion like that, but I think I can trust your cousin to look out for your welfare. I presume there are other ladies who attend the races?"

"Oh, yes, Mother. John Noah says there are lots of women who attend and that it's always a very respectable crowd of people."

The day of the trip came, Eliza was gone for the day, and arrived home late in the day, flushed with excitement. John Noah saw her to the door but did not come in. Eliza came in the house, went looking for her mother, and reported on the day.

"Oh, Mother, It was such fun. The horses were beautiful, and John Noah introduced me to a number of people. He seemed to know everyone there. He bought us sandwiches and lemonade for lunch from a lady who lives near the race track. Again, I had such a good time, Mother! Do you think it's wrong for me to have so much fun so soon after Daddy's death?"

"No, I don't think that at all, Eliza. I think your daddy would have been the last person in the world to think you should sit around moping because he's gone. He would have said something to the effect of 'Dry your eyes, wash your face, and get on with your life.' Besides, I've heard of wives being supposed to mourn for a certain amount of time, but I don't think that applies to daughters."

As the summer progressed, Eliza accompanied John Noah to several races and each time reported that she had experienced a wonderful time. At first, Mary just assumed that the excursions were an attempt by John Noah to cheer up a grieving cousin. The two had grown up together and were first cousins, so Mary thought it a sweet gesture on the young man's part. Toward the end of the summer and especially at threshing time, Mary started to wonder how John Noah had so much time to attend horse races. She also began to suspect there were things about the young man she didn't know. Finally she asked Eliza how John Noah had so much time to attend the races and whether or not he gambled on the horses. The conversation got interesting at that point.

"Mother, I don't know how he has the time to attend the races; he just does, and I don't know if he gambles on the horses."

"Do you see men exchanging money sometimes?"

"Yes, I guess I do."

"What about John Noah?"

"Sometimes he steps away from me for a few minutes. I see him talking to another man, and then he returns to me."

"And do you hear John Noah and the other men talking about the qualities of the horses and which one they expect to win?"

"Yes, sure, it's a race. Why wouldn't they do that?"

"What about John Noah's mood after the race?"

"Sometimes he seems a little grumpy; other times he seems elated. What are you getting at, Mother?"

"I'm getting at the fact that I think your cousin is gambling at these races, and I'm not sure that they're a place where I want you to be."

"Well, I intend to keep going, Mother. It's the first real fun I've had in my adult life, and John Noah is ever so sweet and kind to me."

Mary bit her tongue and didn't say anything more. Her daughter was a grown woman. She did have the right to make her own decisions.

Later, Mary asked John what he knew about his cousin's habits, and John didn't hesitate in giving his mother an honest answer.

"Everybody around here knows he's a gambling man. He frequently brags about how much money he's made on some horse race. Why do you ask?"

"I ask because he has been taking your sister to horse races in Knoxville all summer. She apparently has been having a great time but seems oblivious to the gambling that is probably going on right under her nose."

"Maybe he's just trying to cheer Eliza up because of Dad's death."

"That's what I thought at first. Now I'm not so sure."

When cool weather came, the racing season appeared to have ended, but John Noah continued to come by to see Eliza on a frequent basis. Mary was pretty sure now that the attention being given to Eliza was more than just one cousin trying to cheer up another cousin. She kept her mouth shut and hoped Eliza would figure things out for herself.

Meanwhile, Mary was still very much grieving. There wasn't a day that Cal wasn't on her mind almost constantly. Sometimes she felt like she was in a time warp of some sort. She found herself thinking things like "I need to ask Cal for his opinion on that," and then she would realize that asking Cal for an opinion was no longer an option. Other times when she thought about the love they had shared, she would steal away to her bedroom and shed her tears in private. Occasionally, Hattie allowed five year old Minnie to spend the day with Mary, and she enjoyed those days very much. It was fun to interact with this bright and inquisitive child who reminded her at times of Sarah and offered a welcome distraction from her grief.

A few weeks before Christmas, Mary began to think about a strategy for getting through the holiday. She thought this Christmas, her first without Cal, would likely be especially hard. "Maybe if I surround myself with enough people, I'll be distracted. A family get-together is worth a try."

Plans were made, and several extended family members were invited. Eliza asked for permission to ask John Noah, and he was included without question. Observing interactions on that day, Mary's previous impressions were reinforced. The relationship was definitely more than a cousin-to-cousin friendship.

Mary got through Christmas Day without a major meltdown, and thought to herself that maybe the worst was over. However, the winter days that followed were a constant reminder of what had occurred the previous winter. Each day was a struggle even though she actively sought things she could do to keep her mind occupied. She tried to remember that her children were also missing their father, but she was at a loss as to anything she could do to help them. Both Sarah and John had their spouses and children, and Eliza seemed to have her own focus. Frank was quiet and kept his feelings to himself. Mary finally decided that the only thing she could do was deal with her own emotions.

It was in the spring when Eliza came to her mother with a different kind of request. "Mother, I've never withdrawn any money from my bank account. Is it a big deal?"

"No, it isn't a big deal. Anyone at the bank will be glad to help you. What's going on?"

"John Noah and I want to buy a horse, a yearling."

"Eliza, do you know what you're doing?"

"It's a good looking horse, Mother, and John Noah says its sire has won several races. He thinks it's a good deal."

"I guess my concerns are about more than a horse, but you're a grown woman. I can't tell you how to spend your money, but I wish you'd at least discuss this with your brother John."

"It's none of his business, Mother."

"Okay, I'm going to hush, but I don't think what you're proposing is appropriate. If John Noah wants to buy a horse, let him pay for it himself."

Mary did not inquire later to find out if Eliza helped buy the horse or not. She kept reminding herself that Eliza was soon to be twenty-nine years old.

As it turned out, it was on Eliza's birthday in June that she and John Noah announced their plans to marry. The announcement was made at a family gathering, and Mary said nothing until later. When she did get a chance to speak to Eliza in private, she spoke her piece bluntly.

"Eliza, I have two concerns about this proposed marriage. One, John Noah is your first cousin. More importantly, he's a gambling man, and you know it. I seriously question his ability to support you and any children you may have."

"I love him, Mother, and I intend to marry him. Please don't try to deny me that chance at happiness."

"I've said all I can say, Eliza. Of course I want you to be happy, but don't expect me to be excited about this choice."

On November 28, Eliza was wed to her cousin in the parlor of her parents' home. Mary refused to come downstairs for the wedding.

It was a bleak winter for Mary. She didn't try to plan any kind of Christmas celebration. Lucy had announced just before Christmas that George and his wife wanted her to come live with them. Both Lucy and George had saved their money for the last fifteen years as Cal had suggested, and George had bought a few acres in Jefferson County. He still worked for Mary and John, but he had his own place now. Of course, Mary hated to see Lucy go, but fully understood her desire to be with George and his family.

So now it was just Mary and Frank living in the house. Frank was trying to learn the ropes of farming from John, but Mary sensed that his heart really wasn't in it. On Frank's eighteenth birthday in February, Mary questioned him about what he wanted to do with his life.

"Frank, I sense that farming is not what you want to do with your life. You're eighteen years old, and you have the right to make your own decisions about what you want."

"Dad wanted me to do this, Mother. Half of this beautiful farm will eventually be mine."

"Do not let this farm be a millstone about your neck, son. Your dad wanted to treat you equal to John, and he wanted to make sure I was taken care of."

"I know that, Mother, and I want to honor Dad's wishes. I'm trying to learn the ropes of farming from John."

"You need to accept the fact that John always seemed to like farming. He and George followed your daddy around from the time they were little fellows."

"I know, Mother, but let me try. I have no intention of leaving you here alone."

"I'm not helpless, Frank, and I'm only in my mid-fifties. I've learned a lot about farming since your dad died. You might call me a 'gentleman farmer' except that I'm not a man. You may decide at some point that you want to hire a manager for the farm, or if you don't want to be saddled with it at all, I could buy you out."

"You've become quite the business woman, Mother."

"Sometimes one has no choice, son."

Over time, Mary's acute grief abated, but she never completely stopped missing Cal. Sometimes he appeared in her dreams, always looking like he looked at about the time of their marriage. Each time she had one of those dreams, she usually found herself crying sometime the next day, wishing she could still feel Cal's arms about her in reality instead of a quickly vanishing moment while she slept.

After several years, Frank moved out, finally yielding to his desire to pursue a career in business. Mary was now the sole resident of her home. She tried to fill her time with the garden and her flowers and visiting with Hattie and John. She was fond of all their children but especially their youngest child, born in 1890. He was a handsome lad and seemed to love his grandmother as much as she loved him. In some ways, the boy was almost like an only child because the brother next to him in age was nine years older, and the three older brothers were usually off doing their own thing by the time the youngest arrived on the scene.

Mary treasured her time with this grandchild. He seemed more closely connected to her than all the others, and from the time he was old enough to be allowed out of the house by himself, he often walked the short distance from his parents' house over to visit his grandmother. Although Hattie didn't like it, Mary refused to call him by the name given him at birth. Why had Hattie named him Cedric? It was a name she found in some book about a boy who was an English lord. So Mary called her grandson 'Teddie' even if his mother didn't like it. Indeed, it wasn't the only thing that she and Hattie didn't see eye-to-eye on. Mary also didn't like it that Hattie made the boy wear long curls long after the boy's hair should have been cut.

Petty concerns aside, one nagging worry that Mary had through the years was Eliza's situation. Eliza and John Noah had lived on property owned by his father from the time of their marriage, and occasionally Eliza brought her children over to visit. However, Mary couldn't help but wonder if Eliza had ever fully forgiven her for refusing to attend her wedding. Mary had apologized, and Eliza had said she understood, but still, Mary didn't know if all fences were mended, so to speak. It wasn't until about the time that Eliza was expecting her fourth child that she first said to her mother, "You were right, Mother."

"Right about what?"

"You were right about John Noah. He does have a gambling problem – a big problem. We're broke, Mother, but he won't stop betting on the horses."

"Do you have enough money to buy the food that you can't raise in your garden?"

"I've been using money from my own funds, Mother. That's the only way we've had enough."

"I'm not going to offer you money. I'm afraid it would just wind up in your husband's hands. What I can offer you is a roof over your head if you want to move here with your children."

"Mother, I'm expecting another baby. I'm not ready to throw in the towel yet. John has said he'll stop."

"Do you believe him?"

"I want to believe him, but I guess I don't really."

"Well, let me know if you decide you want to come here."

Two years later, when Eliza was expecting her fifth child, she threw in the proverbial towel and moved with her four children to live with her mother. Her fifth child was born at her mother's home.

In spite of the noise and chaos of little ones under foot, Mary welcomed the children filling her life again. With Eliza's children in her house and John and Hattie's children living a stone's throw away, Mary felt that her life had renewed purpose. She guessed that grandchildren were a reward for living a long life.

Mary's joy at being surrounded by grandchildren was dampened by the loss of daughter Sarah in 1894. Although the family had made an attempt to keep Mary from knowing how ill Sarah was, the return address on Sarah's letters made it clear that she was in some setting being treated for an illness of some sort. On May 10, 1894, Sarah Jane Hughes died of kidney failure. The doctor said that her problem might have originated with an infection she had as a child.

When Mary received the news of Sarah's death, her first thought was how she had prayed that her remaining children would outlive her. Now another one was gone. "Another reason to grieve, another of my children to bury. This one, my precious Sarah, my first born. Now, there are only three left of the seven children I brought into the world. This is a hard burden to carry, but maybe at my age, it won't be many years until I see her again."

Mary went back to trying to fill her time with her grandchildren.

In 1895, Frank married, and Mary suggested that he sell her all rights to his part of the property. He agreed to that arrangement, and all legalities of the matter were quickly settled with the assistance of Alonzo Shields.

The years surrounding the turn of the century brought several changes to the family dynamic. John and Hattie's daughter Minnie married and soon had two little daughters, Helen and Louise. Because they lived in Chattanooga, Mary saw them only on those rare occasions when they came by train for a visit. John's sons Ralph and Calvin decided to seek their fortunes on the west coast. Later, they were followed by their brother Sam. Only Teddie was left in John and Hattie's household. "How strange that their home is already emptying of children," Mary thought. "It doesn't seem like that long since my children were the ones leaving and getting married."

Mary was glad to have the company of Eliza and her brood and her special relationship with young Teddie. Thank heavens his mother had finally allowed him to have his hair cut at age eight. He had shared with his grandmother that he had been in several fights at school over his long curls.

It was Teddie who first mentioned to his grandmother that his parents were talking about following the older sons to the west coast. Mary didn't make much of a response to Teddie about it, but confronted John when she had the opportunity.

"John, Teddie says you're thinking of moving to the west coast. Is that true?"

"Yes, we're thinking about it. Hattie really wants to go. Says she misses the boys."

"What about the farm, John?"

"We'll sell my part. You can hire a manager for your part if you wish. You let Frank out of his obligation; I guess you can let me out of mine."

"I can't legally stop you, John. Your part was always yours, free and clear. The only caveat was that you were supposed to pay rent on your portion. Of course we settled that obligation right after your dad died by having you serve as manager for both sections of the farm. Somehow I sense that there is more to this than what you're saying."

"Well, that's all I'm prepared to say, Mother. I'm sorry; I know this isn't what Dad intended, but he died almost twenty-five years ago. The situation is different now."

"Yes, I'm almost eighty years old for one thing."

"I am sorry, Mother, but my first obligation is to Hattie. It will be a while before we can leave. We have to sell the farm first, and Minnie wants to bring the girls for a visit."

"Was I to be the last to know?"

"I didn't want to upset you, Mother."

"Well, let me know when the sale is. I might want to buy something."

Mary held her tears until she got back in the house. Later she shared the conversation with Eliza and asked if she had been aware of John and Hattie's plans. Eliza admitted that she had known but thought it John's responsibility to tell his mother.

"Is there something I'm missing, Eliza? John said something about his first obligation being to Hattie."

"I don't know for sure, Mother, but I think that Hattie never liked the fact that John didn't get this section of the farm. Then when you bought out Frank's section, John was still managing the entire farm but not getting any extra compensation."

"Managing this section of the farm was in lieu of rent stipulated in your father's will, and if John thought he deserved extra compensation, he could have spoken up."

"He was probably just trying to keep the peace, Mother."

Mary resolved that she would handle this latest heartbreak like she had handled every other heartbreak in her life. She would dry her eyes, wash her face, and get on with her life, however much of it she had left.

Minnie and her two little girls did come for a visit just before John and Hattie left for Oregon. They barely missed being in the great New Market train wreck of 1904 when two trains collided head on. Minnie's original plan was to travel on Saturday, September 24, the day of the wreck, but she had an opportunity to come a day earlier. Shipment of her trunk was delayed however, and it was on one of the trains involved in the wreck. John and Teddie were on their way to New Market with the wagon to pick up the trunk and heard the sound of the massive steam engines colliding. When they got to the scene, they saw splintered wooden passenger cars and a multitude of bodies and body parts strewn about near the crash. When John and Teddie finally returned from their trip, they had to explain the source of the noise which had been heard miles away and the carnage they had witnessed.

Mary was incredibly relieved that Minnie and the children had arrived the day before the wreck but horrified at the thought of so many families that would be mourning. What if Minnie hadn't come a day early? She and her precious little ones could be among the dead. The other horrifying thought that came to Mary's mind was the fact that John, Hattie, and Teddie would soon be traveling all the way to Oregon on a train.

"Once you have children, you can never stop worrying about them, can you?"

After John and Hattie left for Oregon, Mary decided that it was high time that she made a will. She might not have time to make one on her death bed like Cal had done. She had, in fact, planned to leave her section of the farm to John. She thought he deserved it, but he had decided to take a different path. She wasn't about to leave her land to Eliza. She didn't trust Eliza to keep it out of the hands of her husband. No, she would will the farm to Eliza's two teenage sons who were already involved in the operation of the farm but place it in a trust until they were of legal age. She would not include the third son, who seemed to be following in his father's footsteps. What she could do for Eliza was set aside some money in a trust, but she needed to figure out a way to keep it, like the land, out of John Noah's hands.

Eliza's oldest daughter had married and did not appear to be in need of any assistance. The other daughter was preparing to be a teacher. Mary would try to give her a little monetary assistance now. Frank didn't appear to be in need of any assistance either, but

Mary thought she might try to give him something extra for his little daughter, Margaretta. Mary decided that Frank was the logical person to name as executor. He had business skills and could help her set up the trust for Eliza and the two sons.

Mary felt like making her will was the last tangible thing she could do for her children. She had done everything else she knew how to do for them through the years.

Chapter 19

Crossing

Mary lay in her bed and looked around the room. "I came to this room as an eager bride. My marriage was consummated here; all seven of my children were born in this room; and this is where small children crawled into bed with me after middle-of-the-night bad dreams. So many memories! In those days, I never thought about winding up here as a feeble old woman dependent on others for my care. I remember wanting to live to be very old. Back then, I conceived of age merely as years accumulated. I never had the foggiest notion that old age ravages the body and leaves a person handicapped in the ability to enjoy life. I remember puzzling over the Bible verse that speaks to remembering the creator while one is young and before evil days come when one has no pleasure in them. What did 'evil days' mean? Now, I understand."

Until this illness, Mary hadn't spent a day in bed since Frank was born. "My how the years have flown," she thought as her mind took her back to the birth of her last child. It had been an easy delivery, and she had nursed her little one minutes later as Cal sat on the side of the bed and gently stroked her damp hair back from the edge of her face. Cal had always been a little awed by the birth of his children. The last was no different.

Now, here she was, eighty-two years old, her babies long grown except for those who had died. For that matter, most of her grandchildren were grown also. She was grateful to have Eliza and her three youngest children living with her, but she still missed Teddie. Tears welled in her eyes as she remembered how he hugged her goodbye before he left with John and Hattie for Oregon. He had flung his arms around her, hugging her so tight she thought her ribs might break. Then he had suddenly turned her loose and in his deepest voice possible said, "Father says Oregon will be a wonderful place to live." She remembered thinking that Teddie's hug probably conveyed sentiments he couldn't put into words.

As Mary thought about John's family in Oregon, she was pretty sure the place wasn't everything he and Hattie thought it would be. The older sons were not all in one place. One lived hundreds of miles away in

California. Teddie had to drop out of school to help support the family, and for a while both he and his father had worked picking hops. Now Teddie worked at a grocery store in Portland. Once he had enclosed a note with his mother's letter, telling how he had worn out the soles of his shoes walking the streets of Portland, looking for work. The idea of Teddie having to help support the family when he should have been in school made Mary angry. Why wouldn't John admit that he had made a mistake and bring the family back? "Too stubborn," she supposed. She thought about Teddie until she drifted off to sleep for the night.

Eliza came into the room, carrying the breakfast tray. "You're smiling, Mother. Are you having less pain this morning?"

"No, I just had a beautiful dream. I was standing by a river and looking across at a large crowd of people."

"This river?"

"No, not this river. A wide, crystal blue river, and the people on the other side were all smiling at me. Right in front was your daddy, and Mary Elizabeth and

Ellen and Shields, your sister Sarah, both of my parents and everybody I've lost. Even though he was all the way across the river, I could see that twinkle in your daddy's eyes. He looked exactly like he looked when we got married. Then I woke up, and I was still in this room. I wanted to cross the river, but the dream was over."

"I'm glad you had a nice dream, Mother. I have some breakfast for you. Maybe after you eat, you'll feel like sitting up for a bit and looking out the window. We had a beautiful snow last night."

* * * * *

February 3, 1907

My Dear Brother,

Our old mother passed away this morning at 1:00 a.m. She died quietly, like one going to sleep, just a gradual shortening of the breath and heart beats until the end was reached. She has now, in death, as placid and happy expression as you could hope to see. She retained her rational powers until an hour or so before the end came, but could not talk with any comfort for a day or more before her death. I have just talked with Edgar Elmore in Chattanooga, and he has agreed to come up and conduct the funeral tomorrow at one o'clock.

Mother has been confined to the bed nearly all the time for the last three months, and for the last month has suffered much pain. She did not complain of her suffering and only regretted that she had to be waited on. Eliza has been faithful and kind to her during her illness as well as all the family, neighbors and friends. But it is all over now, and she is in the land of the redeemed, reunited with her loved ones who preceded her. May we all so live that when our time comes, we may be permitted to join them in glory is my prayer.

Let me hear from you. With best wishes for you and your family, I am yours truly,

F.T. Nance

[Verbatim letter from Frank Nance to his brother John following the death of their mother, Mary Shields Graham Nance]

369